Q & As
FOR THE
PMBOK®
GUIDE
FIFTH EDITION

Edited by: Frank T. Anbari, PhD, PMP

ISBN: 978-1-935589-85-3

Published by: Project Management Institute, Inc.
                        14 Campus Boulevard
                        Newtown Square, Pennsylvania 19073-3299 USA
                        Phone: +610-356-4600
                        Fax: +610-356-4647
                        Email: customercare@pmi.org
                        Internet: www.PMI.org

PMI Publications welcomes corrections and comments on its
books. Please feel free to send comments on typographical,
formatting, or other errors. Simply make a copy of the relevant
page of the book, mark the error, and send it to: Book Editor, PMI
Publications, 14 Campus Boulevard, Newtown Square, PA 19073-
3299 USA.

To inquire about discounts for resale or educational purposes,
please contact the PMI Book Service Center.

        PMI Book Service Center
        P.O. Box 932683, Atlanta, GA 31193-2683 USA
        Phone: 1-866-276-4764 (within the U.S. or Canada) or
        +1-770-280-4129 (globally)
        Fax: +1-770-280-4113
        Email: info@bookorders.pmi.org

The paper used in this book complies with the Permanent
Paper Standard issued by the National Information Standards
Organization (Z39.48—1984).

10 9 8 7 6 5

Table of Contents

INTRODUCTION

QUESTIONS

ANSWERS

Introduction

In the rapidly growing, fast-changing, and highly competitive world of project management, more and more professionals are recognizing the importance of developing a deeper understanding of the generally accepted knowledge and practice of the project management profession. *Q & As for the PMBOK® Guide Fifth Edition* facilitates this goal by offering multiple choice questions and answers that cover key themes and concepts of project management. This helpful book addresses the project management Knowledge Areas and processes of *A Guide to the Project Management Body of Knowledge (PMBOK® Guide) – Fifth Edition*, the Project Management Institute's global standard. Answers are provided in the back of the book and include references and excerpted text from the *PMBOK® Guide – Fifth Edition*, to enhance the reader's breadth and depth of knowledge. The handy pocket size of *Q & As for the PMBOK® Guide Fifth Edition* makes it convenient to refer to the book anytime, anywhere.

Many people were instrumental in putting together this book and its predecessor publications, *PMBOK Q & A, Q & As for the PMBOK® Guide 2000 Edition, Q & As for the PMBOK® Guide Third Edition,* and *Q & As for the PMBOK® Guide Fourth Edition*. The Project Management Institute (PMI) would like to thank the following contributors to *PMBOK Q & A*: Lewis Ireland, Walter Taylor, Jim Downer, Terry Borovec, Nancy Krajcar, Marylyn Longo, Sue Spengler, Ahmet Taspinar, Joe Abron, Bob Thompson, Francis Hartman, Dana Littlefield, David Overbye, and James Henderson, along with former PMI staff members James S. Pennypacker, Bobby R. Hensley, Toni D. Knott, Allison S. Boone, and Mark S. Parker. PMI would like to thank the following contributors to *Q & As for the PMBOK® Guide 2000 Edition*: Frank T. Anbari and Kate Pechter, along with PMI staff members Steven L. Fahrenkrog, Kristen L. Wright, Richard Schwartz, and Danielle Moore. PMI would also like to thank the following contributors to *Q & As for the PMBOK® Guide Third Edition*: Frank T. Anbari and Donald F. Martin, along with PMI staff members Steven L. Fahrenkrog, Dottie Nichols, Richard Schwartz, and Barbara Walsh. PMI would like to thank the following contributors to *Q & As for the PMBOK® Guide Fourth Edition*: Frank T. Anbari, PhD, PMP (who again provided significant book content and editorial contributions), along with PMI staff members Steven L. Fahrenkrog, John Zlockie, Donn Greenberg, Kristin L. Vitello, Roberta Storer, and Barbara Walsh.

Finally, PMI would like to thank the following contributors to *Q & As for the PMBOK® Guide Fifth Edition*: Frank T. Anbari, PhD, PMP (who again provided significant book content and editorial contributions), along with the following PMI staff members:

John Zlockie • Manager, Standards
Donn Greenberg • Manager, Publications
Kristin L. Vitello, Standards Project Specialist
Roberta Storer • Product Editor
Linda Garber • Copy Editor
Barbara Walsh • Publications Production Supervisor

The PMI team responsible for *Q & As for the PMBOK® Guide Fifth Edition* hopes that you will reinforce your knowledge and enjoy using this updated, expanded, and enhanced project management tool.

Q & As
FOR THE
PMBOK® GUIDE
FIFTH EDITION
Questions

Introduction
(Chapter 1 of the *PMBOK® Guide*)

1. A project is:

A. A set of sequential activities performed in a process or system.

B. A revenue-generating activity that needs to be accomplished while achieving customer satisfaction.

C. An ongoing endeavor undertaken to meet customer or market requirements.

D. A temporary endeavor undertaken to create a unique product, service, or result.

2. Project management is:

A. The integration of the critical path method and the Earned Value Management system.

B. The application of knowledge, skills, tools, and techniques to project activities to meet the project requirements.

C. The application of knowledge, skills, wisdom, science, and art to organizational activities to achieve operational excellence.

D. A subset of most engineering and other technical disciplines.

3. Managing a project typically includes:

A. Balancing the competing project constraints, which include scope, quality, schedule, budget, resources, and risks.

B. Integrating requirements of profitability, low cost, and legal responsibility.

C. Implementation of software, hardware, and other systems to enhance organizational efficiency.

D. Supporting human factors, communications, discipline, and performance management.

4. Portfolio management refers to:

A. Managing various contents of the project file.

B. Managing the levels of financial authority to facilitate project decision making.

C. The centralized management of one or more portfolios to achieve strategic objectives.

D. Applying resource-leveling heuristics across all the organization's projects to achieve the organization's strategic objectives.

5. Project success is measured by:

A. Product and project quality, timeliness, budget compliance, and degree of customer satisfaction.

B. Degree to which the project satisfies its time and budget objectives.

C. The triple constraints of schedule, cost, and technical performance.

D. Degree to which the project satisfies the needs for which it was undertaken and its long-term contribution to aggregate performance of the organization's portfolio.

6. A program is a:

A. Group of related tasks lasting one year or less.

B. Group of related projects, subprograms, and program activities managed in a coordinated way.

C. Project with a cost over $1 million.

D. Sequence of steps constituting a project.

7. **The types of project management office (PMO) structures in organizations include all of the following EXCEPT:**

   A. Supportive PMOs that provide a consultative role to projects by supplying templates, best practices, training, access to information and lessons learned from other projects.

   B. Controlling PMOs that provide support and require compliance through various means.

   C. Harmonizing PMOs that strive to reduce conflict and improve harmony among project team members.

   D. Directive PMOs that take control of the projects by directly managing the projects.

8. **A primary function of a project management office (PMO) is to support project managers in a variety of ways which may include all of the following EXCEPT:**

   A. Delivering specific project objectives and controlling the assigned project resources to best meet objectives of the project.

   B. Managing shared resources across all projects administered by the PMO.

   C. Identifying and developing project management methodology, best practices, and standards.

   D. Coaching, mentoring, training, and oversight.

9. All of the following are true about projects and operations EXCEPT:

A. Operations are ongoing endeavors that produce repetitive outputs, with resources assigned to do basically the same set of tasks according to the standards institutionalized in a product life cycle, whereas projects are temporary endeavors.

B. Projects require project management activities and skill sets, whereas operations require business process management, operations management activities, and skill sets.

C. Projects can intersect with operations at various points during the product life cycle. At each point, deliverables and knowledge are transferred between the project and operations for implementation of the delivered work.

D. Because of their temporary nature, projects cannot help achieve an organization's long-term goals. Therefore, strategic activities in the organization can be generally addressed within the organization's normal operations.

10. **Your job responsibility is to align components (projects, programs, or operations) to the organizational strategy, organized into portfolios or subportfolios to optimize project or program objectives, dependencies, costs, timelines, benefits, resources, and risks. This is known as:**

A. Components management.

B. Process management.

C. Program management.

D. Portfolio management.

11. **In addition to any area-specific skills and general management proficiencies required for the project, effective project management requires that the project manager possess all of the following competencies EXCEPT:**

A. Knowledge, which refers to what the project manager knows about project management.

B. Manipulation, which refers to how the project manager motivates the project team to work hard on the project while working them out of a job.

C. Performance, which refers to what the project manager is able to do or accomplish while applying his or her project management knowledge.

D. Personal, which refers to how the project manager behaves when performing the project or related activity.

12. The *PMBOK® Guide* is the standard for:

A. Managing all projects all of the time across all industries.

B. Managing all projects all of the time across some types of industries.

C. Managing most projects most of the time across many types of industries.

D. Managing some projects some of the time across some types of industries.

Organizational Influences and Project Life Cycle

(Chapter 2 of the *PMBOK® Guide*)

13. Organizational cultures and styles:

A. Are generally similar and manifest in similar ways.

B. Are generally similar but manifest in different ways.

C. Have no impact on a clearly defined project.

D. May have a strong influence on a project's ability to meet its objectives.

14. The project manager has the greatest level of independence and authority in a _____ organization.

A. Strong matrix

B. Weak matrix

C. Projectized

D. Functional

15. The project manager has the lowest level of authority in a _____ organization:

A. Functional

B. Weak matrix

C. Strong matrix

D. Projectized

16. A project coordinator may typically be found in a _____ organization.

A. Projectized

B. Strong matrix

C. Weak matrix

D. Balanced matrix

17. The project manager is more likely to have a full-time role in a _____ organization:

A. Functional

B. Weak matrix

C. Projectized

D. Small capitalization

18. A common title for the project manager's role in a projectized organization is:

A. Project manager.

B. Project coordinator.

C. Project coach.

D. Project expediter.

19. **You are managing a large, complex project with cross-functional project needs. The following organizational structure gives you considerable authority as the project manager:**

A. Balanced matrix organization.

B. Strong matrix organization.

C. Weak matrix.

D. Functional organization.

20. **All of the following statements about the level of authority of the project manager are true EXCEPT:**

A. In a functional organization, the project manager has little or no authority.

B. In weak matrices, the project manager role is more that of a coordinator or expediter than that of a manager.

C. The balanced matrix organization does not provide the project manager with the full authority over the project and project funding.

D. In a strong matrix organization, authority of the project manager is limited.

21. Enterprise environmental factors refer to both internal and external environmental factors that surround or influence a project's success. All of the following are true about these factors EXCEPT:

A. Enterprise environmental factors include organizational culture, structure, and processes.

B. Enterprise environmental factors include government or industry standards, such as regulatory agency regulations, codes of conduct, product standards, quality standards, and workmanship standards.

C. Enterprise environmental factors include project management information systems (e.g., an automated tool, such as a scheduling software tool, a configuration management system, an information collection and distribution system, or web interfaces to other online automated systems).

D. Enterprise environmental factors do not include personnel administration functions (e.g., staffing and retention guidelines, employee performance reviews and training records, reward and overtime policies, and time tracking) because these are considered to be functions of the human resources department.

22. Which of the following is true about functional managers?

A. They are assigned their own permanent staff to carry out the ongoing work, and therefore are not considered to be project stakeholders because of the temporary nature of projects.

B. They are project stakeholders who play a management role within an administrative or functional area of the business.

C. They have a clear directive to manage all tasks within their functional area of responsibility, and therefore they are operational managers and not project stakeholders.

D. They rarely provide subject matter expertise or services to the project.

23. Different or conflicting objectives among project stakeholders:

A. Should be encouraged.

B. Should be ignored.

C. Can make it difficult for project managers to manage stakeholder expectations.

D. Generally make it easy for project managers to manage stakeholder expectations.

24. All of the following are true about project governance EXCEPT:

A. It is an oversight function that is aligned with the organization's governance model and that encompasses the project life cycle.

B. It is a methodology for managing large government projects.

C. It is a framework that provides the project manager and team with structure, processes, decision-making models and tools for managing the project, while supporting and controlling the project for successful delivery.

D. It includes a framework for making project decisions; defines roles, responsibilities, and accountabilities for the success of the project; and determines the effectiveness of the project manager.

25. The collection of generally sequential and sometimes overlapping project phases, whose name and number are determined by the management and control needs of the organization or organizations involved in the project, is known as the:

A. Project waterfall.

B. Project life cycle.

C. Project life stages.

D. Project Management Process Groups.

26. All of the following are true about project phases and the project life cycle EXCEPT:

A. Stakeholder influences, risk, and uncertainty are greatest at the start of the project. These factors decrease over the life of the project.

B. The ability to influence the final characteristics of the project's product, without significantly impacting cost, is highest at the start of the project and decreases as the project progresses toward completion.

C. The cost of changes and correcting errors typically increases substantially as the project approaches completion.

D. Cost and staffing levels are generally steady throughout the project life cycle.

27. All of the following statements about the project life cycle and the product life cycle are true EXCEPT:

A. In the project predictive life cycle, the project scope, and the time and cost required to deliver that scope, are determined as early in the project life cycle as practically possible.

B. In the project iterative and incremental life cycles, project phases intentionally repeat one or more project activities as the project team's understanding of the product increases.

C. The product life cycle is the series of phases that represent the evolution of a product, from concept through delivery, growth, maturity, and to retirement.

D. The product life cycle is contained within the predictive project life cycle.

28. **You are managing a project in which you intend to respond to high levels of change and ongoing stakeholder involvement. The most suitable project life cycle for your project is the:**

A. Predictive life cycle.

B. Adaptive life cycle (also known as the agile method).

C. Waterfall life cycle.

D. Configuration management life cycle.

Project Management Processes
(Chapter 3 of the *PMBOK® Guide*)

29. The five Project Management Process Groups are:

A. Planning, checking, directing, monitoring, and recording.

B. Initiating, planning, executing, monitoring and controlling, and closing.

C. Planning, executing, directing, closing, and commissioning.

D. Initiating, executing, monitoring, evaluating, and closing.

30. Project Management Process Groups are:

A. Overlapping activities that occur throughout the project.

B. Overlapping activities that generally occur at the same level of intensity within each phase of the project.

C. Generally discrete, one-time events.

D. Discrete, repetitive events that occur generally at the same level of intensity throughout each phase of the project.

31. The linkages between Project Management Process Groups are best described by the following:

A. The work breakdown structure links Process Groups.

B. Process Groups are linked by their planned objectives—the summary objective of one often becomes the detailed action plan for another within the project, subproject, or project phase.

C. Process Groups are linked by the outputs that are produced—the output of one process generally becomes an input to another process or is a deliverable of the project, subproject, or project phase.

D. There are no significant links between discrete Process Groups.

32. The relationship between Project Management Process Groups and project life cycle phases is best described by the following:

A. They are unrelated, incompatible concepts.

B. They are the same concept described by different terms to satisfy application area extensions.

C. Phases cross Process Groups such that closing one Process Group provides an input to initiating the next phase.

D. Process Groups interact within each project phase and are normally repeated for each phase.

33. **For a project to be successful, the project team should generally do all of the following EXCEPT:**

A. Comply with requirements to meet stakeholder needs and expectations.

B. Balance the competing constraints of scope, schedule, budget, quality, resources, and risk to produce the specified product, service, or result.

C. Apply knowledge, skills, and processes within the Project Management Process Groups uniformly to meet the project objectives.

D. Select appropriate processes required to meet the project objectives.

34. **All of the following are characteristics of Project Management Process Groups EXCEPT:**

A. Project Management Process Groups are linked by the outputs they produce.

B. The Process Groups are seldom either discrete or one-time events; they are overlapping activities that occur throughout the project.

C. All of the processes are generally needed on all projects, and all of their interactions apply to all projects or project phases conducted in a controlled environment.

D. When a project is divided into phases, the Process Groups are used, as appropriate, to effectively drive the project to completion in a controlled manner.

35. The Initiating Process Group consists of the processes performed to:

A. Define a new project or a new phase of an existing project by obtaining authorization to start the project or phase.

B. Deploy risk mitigation strategies to enhance the likelihood of project success.

C. Establish and describe the need for a project selection process.

D. Approve the market analysis to ensure resolution of potential contract disputes.

36. Performing the Initiating processes at the start of each phase:

A. Is wasteful and should be avoided whenever possible.

B. Helps to keep the project focused on the business need that the project was undertaken to address.

C. Helps to ensure that the project continues regardless of changes in the success criteria.

D. Helps to ensure continuous employment of project team members even if the project is unlikely to satisfy the business need that it was undertaken to address.

37. **Plan quality management to identify quality requirements and/or standards for the project and its deliverables and documenting how the project will demonstrate compliance with quality requirements is part of the:**

A. Conceptual phase.

B. Planning process group.

C. Project implementation phase.

D. Control quality process.

38. **The Control Schedule process for a project:**

A. Focuses on starting the project earlier than scheduled to help mitigate schedule risk and to achieve the approved schedule baseline.

B. Is the process of monitoring the status of project activities to update project progress and manage changes to the schedule baseline to achieve the plan.

C. Is concerned mainly with activities that are on the critical path.

D. Should focus primarily on activities that are difficult to carry out.

39. All of the following processes are performed in the Executing Process Group EXCEPT:

A. Completing the work defined in the project management plan to satisfy the project specifications.

B. Coordinating people and resources in accordance with the project management plan.

C. Managing stakeholder expectations, as well as integrating and performing the activities of the project in accordance with the project management plan.

D. Concluding all activities across all Project Management Process Groups to formally complete appropriate project phases or contractual obligations.

40. The relationship between project management processes and Knowledge Areas is best described by the following:

A. Project management processes are further grouped into separate Knowledge Areas.

B. Knowledge Areas are integrated into project management processes through the project life cycle concept.

C. A Knowledge Area represents a sub-set of concepts, terms, and activities that make up an area of specialization in project management, whereas a project management process is mapped using a data flow diagram.

D. Project teams should utilize the Knowledge Areas and project management processes for all projects all of the time to ensure compliance with project management standards.

Project Integration Management

(Chapter 4 of the *PMBOK® Guide*)

41. Which of the following processes is included in Project Integration Management?

A. Develop project management plan.

B. Control scope definition.

C. Review scope verification.

D. Conduct procurement surveillance.

42. All of the following are characteristics of the project charter EXCEPT:

A. It formally authorizes the existence of a project.

B. Projects are initiated by an entity external to the project. The project initiator or sponsor should be at the level that is appropriate to procure funding and commit resources to the project.

C. It is used primarily to request bids for a project or a specific phase of a project.

D. It provides the project manager with the authority to apply organizational resources to project activities.

43. All of the following are characteristics of the Project Management Information System (PMIS) EXCEPT:

A. It is part of the environmental factors.

B. It provides access to tools, such as a scheduling tool, a work authorization system, a configuration management system, an information collection and distribution system, or interfaces to other online automated systems.

C. It is used as part of the Direct and Manage Project Work.

D. It is used by the project manager and the project management team primarily to generate presentations to key stakeholders.

44. Which of the following is NOT true about tools and techniques of Perform Integrated Change Control?

A. They include expert judgment.

B. They include change control meetings.

C. A change control board (CCB) is responsible for meeting and reviewing the change requests and approving, rejecting, or other disposition of those changes.

D. They include project plan updates.

45. You are managing a $10 million project. Which of the following is an acceptable cause for "re-baselining" this project?

A. The client has approved an addition to the scope of the project with a $150,000 budget increase and a 2-week extension of the scheduled completion.

B. The contractor's company has instituted a Quality Assurance Program in which it has pledged to spend one million dollars during the next year.

C. The productivity in the Design Department is lower than estimated, which has resulted in 1,000 additional hours over what was budgeted and a forecasted 2-week delay of the scheduled completion.

D. The Engineering Department of the performing organization has converted to a new $250,000 CAD system.

46. Configuration control is focused on:

A. The identification and correction of problems arising in functional areas of project implementation.

B. The specification of both the deliverables and the processes; while change control is focused on identifying, documenting, and approving or rejecting changes to the project documents, deliverables, or baselines.

C. Testing new systems.

D. Identifying, documenting and controlling changes to the project and the product baselines, while change control is focused on the specifications of both the deliverables and the processes.

47. A Change Control Board (CCB) is:

A. A formally chartered group of stakeholders responsible for ensuring that only a minimal amount of changes occur on the project.

B. A formal or an informal group of stakeholders that has oversight of project execution.

C. A formally chartered group responsible for reviewing, evaluating, approving, delaying, or rejecting changes to the project, and for recording and communicating such decisions.

D. A dashboard that provides integrated information to help control changes to cost, schedule, and specifications throughout the life of the project.

48. **Some of the configuration management activities included in the Perform Integrated Change Control process include all of the following activities EXCEPT:**

A. Identification and selection of a configuration item to provide the basis for which the product configuration is defined and verified, products and documents are labeled, changes are managed, and accountability is maintained.

B. Monitoring changes in resource leveling heuristics to ensure efficient resource utilization throughout the life cycle of the project.

C. Configuration status accounting, in which information is recorded and reported as to when appropriate data about the configuration item should be provided.

D. Configuration verification and configuration audits that ensure the composition of a project's configuration items is correct and that corresponding changes are registered, assessed, approved, tracked, and correctly implemented.

49. **Actions and activities necessary to transfer the project's products, services, or results to the next phase or to production and/or operations are addressed:**

A. As part of the Close Project or Phase process.

B. Following the plan outlined in the Quality Management process.

C. As requested by senior executives.

D. As the last step in project management.

50. Outputs of the Monitor and Control Project Work process include all of the following EXCEPT:

A. Change requests.

B. Project management plan updates.

C. Work performance reports.

D. Final product, service, or result transition.

Project Scope Management
(Chapter 5 of the *PMBOK® Guide*)

51. **All of the following are true about the project scope management plan EXCEPT:**

    A. It is a component of the project or program management plan.

    B. It describes how the scope will be defined, developed, monitored, controlled, and verified.

    C. It can be formal or informal, broadly framed or highly detailed, based on the needs of the project.

    D. It is not related to the project management plan.

52. Collect Requirements is the process of determining, documenting, and managing stakeholder needs and requirements to meet project objectives. All of the following are true about this process EXCEPT:

A. The project's success is directly influenced by active stakeholder involvement in the discovery and decomposition of needs into requirements and by the care taken in determining, documenting, and managing the requirements of the product, service, or result of the project.

B. Requirements become the foundation of the WBS. Cost, schedule, quality planning, and sometimes procurement are all based upon these requirements.

C. The development of requirements begins with an analysis of the information contained in the project charter, the risk register and the stakeholder management plan.

D. The development of requirements begins with an analysis of the information contained in the project charter, the stakeholder register, and the stakeholder management plan.

53. **You are involved in collecting requirements for your project. You are likely to use the stakeholder register for all of the following EXCEPT:**

A. Identify stakeholders who can provide information on the requirements.

B. Capture major requirements that stakeholders may have for the project.

C. Capture main expectations that stakeholders may have for the project.

D. Evaluate the product breakdown structure (PBS) associated with each of the key stakeholders.

54. **You are developing a document that links product requirements from their origin to the deliverables that satisfy them to help ensure that each requirement adds business value and to manage changes to the product scope. This is known as the:**

A. Configuration management system.

B. Business case.

C. New product development matrix.

D. Requirements traceability matrix.

55. An output of the Define Scope process is:

A. Work breakdown structure (WBS).

B. Resource breakdown structure (RBS).

C. Project scope statement.

D. Scope and schedule delays control plan.

56. All of the following are true about the project scope statement EXCEPT:

A. It is an output of the Validate Scope process.

B. It describes, in detail, the project's deliverables and the work required to create those deliverables.

C. It provides a common understanding of the project scope among project stakeholders.

D. It may contain explicit scope exclusions that can assist in managing stakeholder expectations.

57. Which of the following statements is true about the work breakdown structure (WBS)?

A. The WBS is a hierarchical decomposition of the total scope of work to be carried out by the project team to accomplish the project objectives and create the required deliverables.

B. The WBS is a simple list of project activities in chart form.

C. The WBS is the same as the organizational breakdown structure (OBS).

D. The WBS is the bill of materials (BOM) needed to accomplish the project objectives and create the required deliverables.

58. The following is an example of a constraint associated with the project scope that limits the team's options in scope definition:

A. A predefined budget or any imposed dates or schedule milestones that are issued by the customer or performing organization.

B. The threat of a strike by a subcontractor.

C. Existing relationships with sellers, suppliers, or others in the supply chain.

D. The method used to measure project performance.

59. An input to the Define Scope process is:

A. The type of contract detail language.

B. Project charter.

C. Work breakdown structure (WBS).

D. Decomposition.

60. What is the WBS typically used for?

A. To organize and define the total scope of the project.

B. To identify the logical person to be project sponsor.

C. To define the level of reporting that the seller provides the buyer.

D. As a record of when work elements are assigned to individuals.

61. The following is true about the WBS:

A. The WBS is another term for the bar (Gantt) chart.

B. Each descending level of the WBS represents an increasingly detailed definition of the project work.

C. Work not in the WBS is usually defined in the scope statement of the project.

D. The WBS shows only the critical path activities.

62. Which of the following is true about the Validate Scope process?

A. It is the process of formalizing acceptance of the completed project deliverables.

B. Is not necessary if the project completes on time and within budget.

C. Occurs primarily when revisions or changes are made to project scope.

D. Scope verification is primarily concerned with correctness of the deliverables, whereas quality control is primarily concerned with acceptance of the deliverables and meeting the quality requirements specified for the deliverables.

63. You are managing a global project that involves stakeholders in several international locations. You are likely to consult the WBS dictionary to find:

A. The language translation of technical terms used in the project.

B. Detailed deliverable, activity, and scheduling information about each component in the WBS.

C. Information relating the legal constraints of relevant international locations to the development of the WBS.

D. Strengths, weaknesses, opportunities, and threats (SWOT) of key stakeholders and their impact on the WBS.

64. Which of the following is not an output of the Control Scope process?

A. Work performance information.

B. Change requests.

C. Project documents updates.

D. Accepted deliverables.

65. All of the following are true about the Control Scope process EXCEPT:

A. Control Scope is the process of monitoring the status of the project and product scope and managing changes to the scope baseline.

B. Control Scope is used to manage the actual changes when they occur and is integrated with the other control processes.

C. Scope changes can be avoided by developing clear and concise specifications and enforcing strict adherence to them.

D. Project scope control includes determining the cause and degree of variance relative to the scope baseline and deciding whether corrective or preventive action is required.

Project Time Management
(Chapter 6 of the *PMBOK® Guide*)

66. The Project Time Management processes include:

A. Activity Definition, Activity Sequencing, Activity Execution, Activity Duration Estimation, and Activity Control.

B. Define Activities, Sequence Activities, Estimate Activity Durations, Develop Schedule, and Control Schedule.

C. Identify Activities, Develop Schedule, Execute Activities, Control Activities, and Monitor Schedule Results.

D. Determine Activities, Estimate Activity Durations, Develop Schedule, Implement Activities, and Report Activity Results.

67. In rolling wave planning:

A. Focus is maintained on long-term objectives, allowing near-term objectives to be rolled out as part of the ongoing wave of activities.

B. The work to be accomplished in the near term is planned in detail, whereas the work in the future is planned at a higher level.

C. The work far in the future is planned in detail for work packages that are at a low level of the WBS.

D. A wave of detailed activities is planned during strategic planning to ensure that WBS deliverables and project milestones are achieved.

68. The Precedence Diagramming Method (PDM) is:

A. A technique in which activities are represented by nodes and are graphically linked by one or more logical relationships to show the sequence in which the activities are to be performed.

B. A method that uses a probabilistic approach to scheduling project activities.

C. A time-phased graphical representation of the arrow diagramming method (ADM) and shows durations of project activities as well as their dependencies.

D. More accurate than the critical path method for scheduling when there are uncertainties about the durations of project activities.

69. The duration of the activity is affected by all of the following EXCEPT:

A. The estimated activity resource requirements.

B. The types of resources assigned to the activity.

C. The availability of the resources assigned to the activity.

D. Using the precedence diagramming method (PDM) for scheduling activities instead of using the critical path method (CPM).

70. **A schedule compression technique used to shorten the schedule duration for the least incremental cost by adding resources is called:**

A. Crashing.

B. Program evaluation and review technique (PERT).

C. Precedence diagramming method (PDM).

D. Fast tracking.

71. **The "fast tracking" method of schedule compression involves:**

A. The use of industrial engineering techniques to improve productivity, thereby finishing the project earlier than originally planned.

B. Performing in parallel for at least a portion of their duration activities or phases that are normally done in sequence, which may result in rework and increased risk.

C. Going on a "mandatory overtime schedule" to complete the project on schedule or earlier if possible.

D. Assigning "dedicated teams" to critical path activities to achieve project schedule objectives.

72. An example of a mandatory dependency is:

A. A dependency established based on knowledge of best practices within a particular application area.

B. A dependency established based on some unusual aspect of the project where a specific sequence is desired.

C. On a construction project, to erect the superstructure only after the foundation has been built.

D. On a software development project, to start design only after completion and approval of all project requirements.

73. Inputs to the Define Activities process are:

A. Schedule management plan, work breakdown structure, project schedule, and network diagram.

B. Project schedule, resource estimates, progress reports, and change requests.

C. Scope management plan, project network diagram, constraints, and assumptions.

D. Schedule management plan, scope baseline, enterprise environmental factors, and organizational process assets.

74. Bar charts show:

A. The level of effort for an activity.

B. Availability of resources assigned to perform project activities.

C. Activity start and end dates, as well as expected durations.

D. Relative priority of activities.

75. The Precedence Diagramming Method (PDM) shows:

A. Various levels of the work breakdown structure.

B. Activities likely to be involved in project integration and resource allocation processes.

C. The logical relationships that exist between activities.

D. The project completion date based on normal resource availability.

76. The critical path is established by calculating the following dates:

A. Start-to-start, start-to-finish, finish-to-finish, finish-to-start.

B. Early start, early finish, late start, late finish.

C. Predecessor-to-successor, predecessor-to-predecessor, successor-to-successor.

D. Primary-to-secondary, primary-to-finish, secondary-to-secondary, finish-to-finish.

77. All of the following are true about resource leveling EXCEPT:

A. It can be used to keep resource usage at a constant level during certain time periods.

B. It can often cause the original critical path to change, usually to increase.

C. It is used to develop a resource-based WBS.

D. It is a resource optimization technique that can be used to adjust the schedule model due to demand and supply of resources.

78. The following is true about the critical chain method (CCM):

A. It is a schedule network analysis technique that accounts for limited resources and project uncertainties.

B. It is a network scheduling technique that allows the development of an optimum project schedule when resources are unlimited.

C. It is another name for the resource-loaded bar chart.

D. It is primarily used to ensure the safety of critical stakeholders in major construction projects.

79. **All of the following choices represent inputs to the Estimate Activity Resources process EXCEPT:**

   A. Activity list.

   B. Enterprise environmental factors.

   C. The deliverable-oriented WBS of a previous, similar project.

   D. Organizational process assets.

80. **Outputs from the Estimate Activity Resources process include:**

   A. Job descriptions of resources required for the project.

   B. Salary schedules for various project human resources.

   C. Identification of the types and quantities of resources required for each activity in a work package.

   D. Analogous estimates of resource requirements for each work package and each work period.

81. As one of the tools and techniques of the Sequence Activities process, a lead:

A. Directs a delay in the successor activity.

B. Could be accomplished by a finish-to-start relationship with a delay time.

C. Means that the successor activity cannot start until after the predecessor is completed.

D. Is the amount of time whereby a successor activity can be advanced with respect to a predecessor activity.

82. Program Evaluation and Review Technique (PERT) uses:

A. The weighted average of the triangular or beta distributions duration estimates to calculate the activity early finish date when there is uncertainty with the individual activity estimates.

B. The weighted average of optimistic, pessimistic, and most likely estimates to calculate the expected duration of the activity.

C. Dummy activities to represent logic links among three or more activities.

D. Free float instead of total float in the schedule calculations.

83. Analogous duration estimating is:

A. Frequently used to estimate project duration when there is a limited amount of detailed information about the project.

B. A bottom-up estimating technique.

C. Based on multiple duration estimating.

D. Generally more accurate than other duration estimating methods when expert judgment is used.

84. The critical chain:

A. Focuses on managing the resources applied to the project buffer and feeding buffer activities.

B. Adjusts the required dependencies in the project schedule to optimize resource constraints.

C. Adds duration buffers that are work schedule activities to manage risk and maintains focus on the total float of network paths.

D. Adds duration buffers that are non-work schedule activities to manage uncertainty and focuses on managing the remaining buffer durations against the remaining durations of chains of activities.

85. **Consider the following three estimates for the duration of an activity:**
   Optimistic (tO) = 4 weeks
   Most likely (tM) = 5 weeks
   Pessimistic (tP) = 9 weeks

   Using the beta distribution and the traditional Program Evaluation and Review Technique (PERT), the calculated Expected activity duration (tE) is:

   A. 4.0 weeks.

   B. 4.5 weeks.

   C. 5.5 weeks.

   D. 6.5 weeks.

86. **Consider the following information about the duration of an activity:**
   Calculated expected (tE) = 5 weeks
   Optimistic (tO) = 4 weeks
   Pessimistic (tP) = 8 weeks

   Using the beta distribution and the traditional Program Evaluation and Review Technique (PERT), the most likely (tM) activity duration is:

   A. 4.0 weeks.

   B. 4.5 weeks.

   C. 5.0 weeks.

   D. 6.0 weeks.

87. **Consider the following three estimates for the duration of an activity:**
    Optimistic (tO) = 6 weeks
    Most likely (tM) = 9 weeks
    Pessimistic (tP) = 15 weeks

    Using the triangular distribution, the calculated Expected activity duration (tE) is:

    A. 10.0 weeks.

    B. 10.5 weeks.

    C. 11.5 weeks.

    D. 12.0 weeks.

88. **An activity in a project network has the following characteristics: ES = 5, EF = 10, and LF = 14. Therefore, LS = _____.**

    A. 9.0 weeks.

    B. 10.0 weeks.

    C. 11.0 weeks.

    D. 12.0 weeks.

89. **An activity in a network has the following characteristics: ES = 12, EF = 22, and LS = 14. ES and LS relate to the beginning of the week whereas EF relates to the end of the week. The duration of the activity is:**

A. 8.0 weeks.

B. 11.0 weeks.

C. 12.0 weeks.

D. 14.0 weeks.

90. **"Crashing" in time management is:**

A. A schedule compression technique used to shorten the schedule duration for the least incremental cost by adding resources.

B. A schedule compression technique in which phases or activities that are normally done in sequence are performed in parallel.

C. The timely input of data to calculate the critical path.

D. Equivalent to minimizing float in the project schedule network.

Consider the following schedule network that shows the activities in your project and their associated durations in days for questions 91–92:

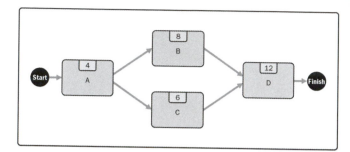

91. The critical path in this network is:

    A. A-B-C.

    B. A-B-D.

    C. A-C-D.

    D. A-B-C-D.

92. The free float for activity C is:

    A. +4.

    B. +2.

    C. 0.

    D. −2.

Project Cost Management

(Chapter 7 of the *PMBOK® Guide*)

93. Project Cost Management includes all of the following processes EXCEPT:

A. Plan cost management.

B. Level resources.

C. Determine budget.

D. Control costs.

94. The cost management plan has all of the following characteristics EXCEPT:

A. It is based on project cost estimates and is separate from the project management plan.

B. It may specify variance thresholds for monitoring cost performance to indicate an agreed-upon amount of variation to be allowed before some action needs to be taken.

C. It may specify the level of precision, which is the degree to which activity cost estimates will be rounded up or down.

D. It describes how the project costs will be planned, structured, and controlled.

95. All of the following are true about cost estimates EXCEPT:

A. Cost estimates are generally expressed in units of some currency (i.e., dollars, euros, yen, etc.), although in some instances other units of measure, such as staff hours or staff days, are used to facilitate comparisons by eliminating the effects of currency fluctuations.

B. Costs are estimated for all resources that will be charged to the project.

C. Information in the risk register should not be considered in cost estimates, because risks can be either threats or opportunities and their impact tends to balance out.

D. A cost estimate is a quantitative assessment of the likely costs for resources required to complete the activity. Cost estimates may be presented at the activity level or in summary form.

96. An activity cost estimate includes all of the following resource categories EXCEPT:

A. Labor.

B. Materials.

C. Equipment.

D. Time shortages.

97. Parametric estimating involves:

A. Defining cost or duration parameters of the project life cycle.

B. Calculating individual cost estimates for each work package and integrating them to obtain the total cost of the project.

C. Using a statistical relationship between relevant historical data and other variables to calculate a cost estimate for project work.

D. Using the actual cost of a previous similar project to estimate the cost of the current project.

98. Analogous cost estimating:

A. Integrates bottom-up estimating techniques with relevant statistical relationships to estimate the cost of the current project.

B. Relies on the actual cost of previous, similar projects as the basis for estimating the cost of the current project.

C. Is used most frequently in the later phases of a project.

D. Summarizes estimates for individual work packages to estimate the cost of the current project.

99. Which of the following represents processes concerned with establishing and controlling the cost baseline?

A. Plan Resources and Contain Costs.

B. Estimate Costs, Develop Budget, and Adhere to Baseline.

C. Determine Budget and Control Costs.

D. Resource Planning, Cost Estimating, and Cost Control.

100. The cost performance baseline has all of the following characteristics EXCEPT:

A. It is the approved version of the time-phased project budget, excluding any management reserves, and is used as a basis for comparison with actual results.

B. It shows the actual cost expenditures throughout the project life cycle.

C. It is developed as a summation of the approved budgets for the different schedule activities.

D. It is typically displayed in the form of an S-curve.

101. Project cost control includes all of the following EXCEPT:

A. Informing appropriate stakeholders of all approved changes and associated cost.

B. Monitoring cost performance to isolate and understand variances from the approved cost baseline.

C. Influencing the factors that create changes to the authorized cost baseline.

D. Allocating the overall estimates to individual work packages to establish a cost baseline.

102. **You have been promoted to the position of project manager for a large project, due to the abrupt transfer of the previous project manager. On the first day in your new, exciting position, you find a folder on your desk entitled: Earned Value Management. In that folder, you find only the following chart related to your project with the Data Date of a few days ago:**

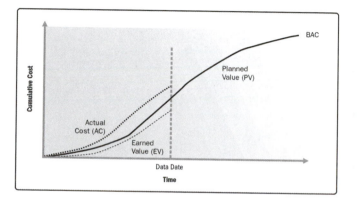

Based on this chart you conclude that:

A. The project is below budget and probably ahead of schedule.

B. The project is over budget and probably behind schedule.

C. The project is below budget but probably behind schedule.

D. The performance on this project compared with budget and schedule cannot be determined because this chart does not show any values.

Cumulative data for questions 103–108:

BAC = 200

PV = 100

AC = 120

EV = 80

103. Assuming that all future work will be performed at the budgeted rate, the estimate at completion (EAC) is:

   A. 200.

   B. 220.

   C. 240.

   D. 260.

104. Assuming that what the project has experienced to date can be expected to continue in the future, the estimate at completion (EAC) is:

   A. 300.

   B. 325.

   C. 350.

   D. 375.

105. **Assuming that future work will be performed at an efficiency rate that considers both the cost and schedule performance indices because project schedule is a factor that impacts future effort, the estimate at completion (EAC) is:**

   A. 250.

   B. 300.

   C. 350.

   D. 345.

106. **Assuming that what the project has experienced to date can be expected to continue in the future, the variance at completion (VAC) is:**

   A. −80.

   B. −100.

   C. +100.

   D. +200.

107. Assuming that all future work will be performed at the budgeted rate, the estimate to complete (ETC) is:

A. 120.

B. 140.

C. 180.

D. 200.

108. Your sponsor specifies that there is no additional money in the budget for your project and asks you to complete the project at the original budget at completion (BAC). To achieve that goal, you and your team must complete the remaining work at the to-complete performance index (TCPI) of:

A. 0.67.

B. 1.00.

C. 1.50.

D. 2.00.

109. **The estimate at completion (EAC) is typically based on:**

   A. The actual costs incurred for work completed (AC), and the estimate to complete (ETC) the remaining work.

   B. The actual costs incurred for work completed (AC) and the cumulative cost performance index (CPI).

   C. The earned value (EV) and the actual cost for work completed (AC).

   D. The cost performance index (CPI) and the cost variance (CV).

110. **Your earned value management analysis indicates that your project is falling behind its baseline schedule. You know this because the cumulative EV is much:**

   A. Higher than the cumulative AC.

   B. Higher than the cumulative PV.

   C. Lower than the cumulative PV.

   D. Lower than the cumulative CPI.

111. **Which of the following cumulative measures indicates that your project is about 9% under budget?**

   A. The cumulative AC was 100, and the cumulative EV was 110.

   B. The cumulative PV was 100, and the cumulative AC was 110.

   C. The cumulative AC was 110, and the cumulative EV was 100.

   D. The cumulative EV was 100, and the cumulative PV was 110.

112. **Earned value management (EVM) is a commonly used:**

   A. Analysis of the value of the equipment that has been installed in the project as of the status date.

   B. Analysis of the sum of the labor costs, which have been incurred on the project to date.

   C. Method of performance measurement for projects.

   D. Method of measuring the amount of money that has been spent on the project to date.

113. During the sixth monthly update on a ten-month, $300,000 project, analysis of the earned value management data shows that the cumulative PV is $190,000, the cumulative AC is $120,000, and the cumulative EV is $150,000. In planning its action, the project management team can conclude all of the following from these measures EXCEPT:

A. Less has been accomplished than was planned.

B. Less has been spent than planned.

C. Continuing performance at the same efficiency with no management intervention, the project will probably be completed behind schedule and under budget.

D. Continuing performance at the same efficiency with no management intervention, the project will probably be completed ahead of schedule and over budget.

114. In earned value management, the cost variance is equal to:

A. EV minus PV.

B. EV minus AC.

C. AC minus EV.

D. PV minus EV.

115. **Earned value (EV) involves all of the following EXCEPT:**

A. Value of the work performed expressed in terms of the budget authorized for that work.

B. Actual cost for an activity or work breakdown structure (WBS) component.

C. Progress measurement criteria, which should be established for each WBS component to measure work in progress.

D. Budget associated with the authorized work that has been completed.

116. **If cumulative PV = 100, cumulative EV = 98, and cumulative AC = 104, the project is likely to be:**

A. Ahead of schedule.

B. Headed for a cost overrun.

C. Operating at project cost projections.

D. Under budget at completion.

Cumulative data for questions 117–118:

Item	PV	AC	EV
1	10,000	11,000	10,000
2	9,000	8,000	7,000
3	8,000	8,000	8,000
4	7,000	7,000	5,000

117. Which item is MOST over budget?

A. Item 1

B. Item 2

C. Item 3

D. Item 4

118. Which item has the LOWEST SPI?

A. Item 1

B. Item 2

C. Item 3

D. Item 4

Project Quality Management

(Chapter 8 of the *PMBOK® Guide*)

119. **Project Quality Management includes the processes and activities of the performing organization that determine quality policies, objectives, and responsibilities so that:**

    A. The project will satisfy the needs for which it was undertaken.

    B. Process capability will be improved.

    C. Products, services, and results will be controlled.

    D. Project team performance will meet standards.

120. **Quality and grade are not the same. A fundamental distinction is that:**

    A. Quality as a delivered performance or result is the degree to which a set of inherent characteristics fulfill requirements; grade as a design intent is a category assigned to deliverables having the same functional use but different technical characteristics.

    B. A quality level that fails to meet quality requirements may not be a problem; a low grade of quality is always a problem.

    C. Delivering the required levels of quality is not included in the responsibilities of the project manager and the project team.

    D. Delivering the required levels of grade is not included in the responsibilities of the project manager and the project team.

121. Understanding, evaluating, defining, and managing requirements are essential to satisfying:

A. Customer expectations.

B. The scope statement.

C. Upper management.

D. Functional requirements.

122. Modern quality management approaches recognize the importance that quality:

A. Is planned, built, and inspected into the product, service, or result.

B. Quality does not cost to plan and implement into the project.

C. Should be planned, designed, and built into—not inspected into the project's management or the project's deliverables.

D. Requires constant, vigilant inspection.

123. All of the following are primary benefits of meeting quality requirements EXCEPT:

A. Less rework.

B. Higher productivity.

C. Lower costs.

D. Fewer change orders.

124. Inputs to quality control include all of the following EXCEPT:

A. Project management plan.

B. Quality checklists.

C. Work performance data.

D. PERT chart.

125. Design of experiments (DOE) is a statistical method used to:

A. Determine how various elements of a project interrelate.

B. Identify which factors may influence specific variables of a product or process under development or in production.

C. Establish a standard by which to measure project performance.

D. Compare actual or planned project practices with those of other projects.

126. **The quality management plan is a component of the _____ that describes how the organization's quality policies will be implemented.**

A. Project management plan.

B. WBS.

C. Project scope.

D. External project stakeholders' management plan.

127. **Perform Quality Assurance is the process of:**

A. Applying planned, systematic quality activities to ensure effective policing and conformance of the project team to the approved specifications.

B. Providing the project team and stakeholders with standards by which project performance is measured.

C. Auditing the quality requirements and the results from quality control measurements to ensure that appropriate quality standards and operational definitions are used.

D. Assuring the implementation of appropriate specifications, which generally reduces the probability of the project being completed on schedule.

128. A _____ is a special form vertical bar chart used to identify the vital few sources that are responsible for causing most of a problem's effects.

A. PERT chart.

B. Bar chart.

C. Network diagram.

D. Pareto diagram.

129. Cost of quality includes all of the following EXCEPT:

A. Preventing nonconformance to requirements.

B. Appraising the product or service for conformance to requirements.

C. Failing to meet requirements (rework).

D. Operating computers required for the project.

130. **Because of the temporary nature of and the potential benefits that may be derived from reducing the post-project cost of quality, _____ may choose to invest in product quality improvement, especially in the areas of prevention and appraisal:**

A. Sponsoring organizations.

B. The project management team.

C. The project executive management team.

D. The project quality function deployment (QFD) organization.

131. **The seven basic quality tools include all of the following EXCEPT:**

A. Flowcharts.

B. Pareto diagrams.

C. Control charts.

D. Quality control tendency charts.

132. Control charts have all of the following characteristics EXCEPT:

A. They are used to determine whether or not a process is stable or has predictable performance.

B. They can be used to monitor various types of output variables.

C. They are used to illustrate how various factors might be linked to potential problems or effects.

D. They are graphical displays of process data over time and against established control limits, which has a centerline that assists in detecting a trend of plotted values toward either control limit.

133. Consider the following control chart for a repetitive process:

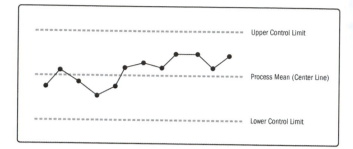

Based on this chart you conclude that the process is:

A. Considered out of control because seven consecutive plot points are above the mean.

B. Considered in control because no data points exceed the control limits.

C. Undergoing continuous improvement because it indicates a positive trend.

D. In an unspecified control status because the upper and lower control limits are different from specification limits, which are based on requirements of the agreement.

134. **Perform Quality _____ is the process of auditing the quality requirements and the results from quality control measurements to ensure that appropriate quality standards and operational definitions are used.**

    A. Planning.

    B. Assurance.

    C. Improvement.

    D. Benchmarking.

135. **In using cost-benefit analysis in the Plan Quality Management process it can be noted that:**

    A. The primary benefit of meeting quality requirements is the reduced cost associated with project quality management activities.

    B. The primary benefits of meeting quality requirements include less rework, higher productivity, lower costs, increased stakeholder satisfaction, and increased profitability.

    C. The primary cost of meeting quality requirements is the increased rework to ensure stakeholder satisfaction.

    D. Quality cost cannot be evaluated in relationship to the expected benefit of quality in a given project.

136. **Benchmarking involves comparing actual or planned project practices to those of comparable projects with all of the following characteristics EXCEPT:**

A. To identify best practices and generate ideas for improvement.

B. To provide a basis for measuring performance.

C. Within the performing organization or outside of it.

D. Within the same application area but not in a different application area.

137. **All of the following are true about Six Sigma and Lean Six Sigma EXCEPT:**

A. It is a quality improvement initiative undertaken by the performing organization.

B. It could improve the quality of the project's management.

C. It could improve the quality of the project's product.

D. It focuses on systematically correcting defects, errors, or mistakes revealed by inspection.

138. The basis for continuous quality improvement is the:

A. Plan-do-check-act (PDCA) cycle as defined by Shewhart and modified by Deming.

B. Process decision program chart (PDPC).

C. Ready-aim-fire (RAF) cycle linked by results.

D. Conceptualize-design-execute-finish (CDEF) cycle.

139. All of the following are true about affinity diagrams EXCEPT:

A. They are used to identify the key issues and the suitable alternatives to be prioritized as a set of decisions for implementation.

B. They are similar to mind-mapping techniques.

C. They are used to generate ideas that can be linked to form organized patterns of thought about a problem.

D. They can be used in project management to give structure to the decomposition of scope and enhance the creation of the WBS.

140. Which of the following is true regarding precision and accuracy?

A. Precision is a measure of correctness, whereas accuracy is an assessment of exactness.

B. Precision is a measure of exactness, whereas accuracy is an assessment of correctness.

C. Precision and accuracy are essentially the same.

D. As an example, points clustered tightly in one area of the target but not in the bull's eye are considered to have high accuracy, whereas points that are more spread out but equidistant from the bull's eye are considered to have the same degree of precision.

Project Human Resource Management
(Chapter 9 of the *PMBOK® Guide*)

141. The major processes of Project Human Resource Management are:

A. Leadership, Management, Team Building, and Negotiation.

B. Develop Project Staffing Plan, Recruit Project Team, Administer Personnel Actions, and Manage Labor Relations.

C. Plan Organizational Structure, Build Project Team, Develop Communications Plan, and Manage Team Conflicts.

D. Plan Human Resource Management, Acquire Project Team, Develop Project Team, and Manage Project Team.

142. The responsibility assignment matrix (RAM) is:

A. Used for development of the project budget and network diagrams.

B. Developed at the activity level and used to closely link project roles and responsibilities to project network activities.

C. Used to illustrate the connections between work packages or activities and project team members. It ensures that there is only one person accountable for any one task to avoid confusion of responsibility.

D. Used to identify accountabilities and responsibilities in individual performance appraisals of project team members.

143. The Human Resource Management Plan should generally include all of the following EXCEPT:

A. Roles and responsibilities.

B. Project organization charts.

C. Staffing management plan.

D. Project interfaces.

144. Questions that arise when planning the acquisition of project team members generally include all of the following EXCEPT:

A. Whether the human resources come from within the organization or from external, contracted sources.

B. The costs associated with each level of expertise needed for the project.

C. The compensation of senior executives.

D. The level of assistance that the organization's human resource department and functional managers are able to provide to the project management team.

145. A resource histogram has all of the following characteristics EXCEPT:

A. It is generally used by the project management team to show the project sponsor and other key stakeholders that the project has insufficient resources to be completed on schedule.

B. It is a tool for charting human resources used as a means of providing a visual representation or resources allocation to all interested parties, as part of the staffing management plan.

C. It illustrates the number of hours a person, department, or entire project team that will be needed each week or month over the course of the project.

D. It can include a horizontal line that represents the maximum number of hours available from a particular resource. Bars that extend beyond the maximum available hours identify the need for a resource optimization strategy.

146. The Acquire Project Team is the process the process of confirming human resource availability and obtaining the team necessary to complete project activities. The enterprise environmental factors that can influence this process generally include all of the following EXCEPT:

A. Organizational structure.

B. Political philosophy.

C. Competency levels, prior experience, and cost rate.

D. Personnel administration policies, such as those that affect outsourcing.

147. **It is important that the staffing management plan addresses how team members will be released when they are no longer needed on the project for all of the following reasons EXCEPT:**

A. To reduce project costs.

B. To improve morale when smooth transitions to upcoming projects are already planned.

C. To optimize the utilization of enterprise material resources.

D. To help mitigate human resource risks that may occur during or at the end of a project.

148. **To be effective, recognition and rewards systems should have the following characteristics EXCEPT:**

A. Clear criteria for rewards and a planned system for their use to help promote and reinforce desired behaviors.

B. Be based on activities and performance under a person's control.

C. Cultural differences should be considered when determining recognition and rewards.

D. The required performance for rewards should be made unachievable for most team members, to ensure that all team members strive for excellence throughout the project.

149. Tools and techniques to acquire the project team include all of the following EXCEPT:

A. Pre-assignment.

B. Acquisition.

C. Staffing management plan.

D. Negotiation.

150. Co-location is one of the tools and techniques used to:

A. Plan the organizational structure.

B. Develop the project team.

C. Acquire the project team.

D. Control project human resources.

151. All of the following are true about conflict management EXCEPT:

A. It is inevitable in a project environment and should be addressed early.

B. It should be addressed usually in private.

C. It should be addressed only when it becomes disruptive and at a special team meeting.

D. It should be addressed using a direct, collaborative approach.

152. Team building has all of the following characteristics EXCEPT:

A. Team-building activities can vary from a 5-minute agenda item in a status review meeting to an off-site, professionally facilitated experience designed to improve interpersonal relationships.

B. Team-building should be primarily considered after major conflicts within the project team, because they generally waste precious resource time and cause schedule delays.

C. Team-building strategies are particularly valuable when team members operate from remote locations without the benefit of face-to-face contact.

D. Team-building is essential during the front end of a project and is an ongoing process. To effectively manage inevitable changes in the project environment, a continued or renewed team-building effort is required.

153. **Training has all of the following characteristics EXCEPT:**

    A. It includes all activities designed to enhance the competencies of the project team members.

    B. It can be formal or informal. Examples of training methods include classroom, online, computer-based, on-the-job training from another project team member, mentoring, and coaching.

    C. If project team members lack necessary management or technical skills, the project should be deemed outside the core competencies of the performing organization, outsourced, or abandoned.

    D. If project team members lack the necessary management or technical skills, such skills can be developed as part of the project work.

154. **Effective team development strategies and activities are expected to increase the team's performance, which increases the likelihood of meeting project objectives. The evaluation of a team's effectiveness may include all of the following indicators EXCEPT:**

    A. Improvements in skills that allow individuals to perform assignments more effectively.

    B. Improvements in competencies that help the team perform better as a team.

    C. Improvements in the overall project performance as a result of increased intensity of conflict among project team members.

    D. Reduced staff turnover rate.

155. In many projects, negotiation is:

A. Primarily the concern of contract administration.

B. An integral part of project management and likely for staff assignments.

C. A direct result of ineffective decision making.

D. Conducted by senior executives to increase the probability of project success.

156. Generally acknowledged techniques for resolving conflict include:

A. Smooth, compromise, collaborate, and co-locating.

B. Accept, compromise, attack, and separate.

C. Accommodate, compromise, force, and collaborate.

D. Withdraw, force, elaborate, and provide sensitivity training.

157. Managing and leading the project team include:

A. Being aware of, subscribing to, and ensuring that all team members follow professional and ethical behaviors.

B. Subscribing to the code of professional conduct but does not involve ensuring that all team members follow professional and ethical behaviors.

C. Influencing the project team to achieve the triple constraints of the project. However, professional and ethical behaviors of project team members are outside the domain of the project management team.

D. Instructing the project team to avoid being caught in repetitive violations of the norms of professional and ethical behaviors specified by the performing organization.

158. All of the following are true about organizational theory EXCEPT:

A. Organizational theory provides information regarding the way in which people, teams, and organizational units behave.

B. Applicable organizational theories may recommend exercising a flexible leadership style that adapts to the changes in a team's maturity level throughout the project life cycle.

C. Effective use of common themes identified in organizational theory can shorten the amount of time, cost, and effort needed to create the Plan Human Resource Management process outputs and improve planning efficiency.

D. Skillful use of common themes identified in organizational theory can help the project manager in manipulating project team members and other project stakeholders to achieve professional and personal gains.

159. Team development stages include:

A. Starting, organizing, preparing, executing, and closing.

B. Forming, storming, norming, performing, and adjourning.

C. Acquiring, managing, leading, decision making, and releasing.

D. Initiating, planning, executing, monitoring and controlling, and closing.

160. **Examples of interpersonal skills that a project manager uses most often include all of the following indicators EXCEPT:**

A. Leadership.

B. Influencing.

C. Biasing.

D. Effective decision making.

Project Communications Management

(Chapter 10 of the *PMBOK® Guide*)

161. The major processes of Project Communications Management are:

A. Plan Communications Management, Manage Communications, and Control Communications.

B. Plan Communications Management, Develop Responses, Report Progress, and Distribute Information.

C. Plan Communications, Distribute Information, and Schedule Reporting.

D. Distribute Information, Report Changes, Update Project Documents, and Accept Project Deliverables.

162. Inputs to the Plan Communications Management process include:

A. Project management plan, stakeholder register, enterprise environmental factors, and organizational process assets.

B. Stakeholder requirements, project scope statement, project budget, and project schedule.

C. Organizational structure, stakeholder analysis, project management plan, and communications barriers.

D. Stakeholder management strategy, RAM, WBS, and administrative procedures.

163. The communications management plan usually contains all of the following EXCEPT:

A. Information to be communicated, including language, format, content, and level of detail.

B. Time frame and frequency for the distribution of required information and receipt of acknowledgment or response, if applicable.

C. Methods or technologies used to convey the information, such as memos, email, and/or press releases.

D. Email archives, correspondence, reports, and documents related to the project from all stakeholders.

164. Hard-copy document management, electronic communications management, and web interfaces to scheduling and project management software are examples of:

A. Integrated project management information systems (IPMIS).

B. Internal communications systems.

C. Information management systems.

D. Project records.

165. **Factors that can affect the choice of communication technology generally include all of the following EXCEPT:**

A. Urgency of the need for information.

B. Availability of technology.

C. Executive requirements.

D. Sensitivity and confidentiality of the information.

166. **Performance reporting is the act of collecting and distributing performance information, generally including all of the following EXCEPT:**

A. Status reports.

B. Decision tree analysis.

C. Progress measurements.

D. Forecasts.

167. **As part of the communications process, the sender is responsible for:**

A. Ensuring that the receiver agrees with the message.

B. Confirming that the communication is correctly understood.

C. Presenting the information in the most favorable manner.

D. Decoding the medium correctly.

168. As part of the communications process, the receiver is responsible for:

A. Agreeing with the sender's message.

B. Pretending that the message is received only partially, to encourage further discussions.

C. Ensuring that the information is received in its entirety, understood correctly, and acknowledged or responded to appropriately.

D. Specifying that a verbal message does not give insight to problem areas, and requiring that the message be reduced to writing to avoid potential confusion.

169. Sources of information typically used to identify and define project communication requirements include all of the following EXCEPT:

A. Project organization and stakeholder responsibility relationships.

B. Disciplines, departments, and specialties involved in the project.

C. Logistics of how many persons will be involved with the project and at which locations.

D. Availability of in-place technology at the project location.

170. **Performance reporting involves the periodic collection and analysis of baseline versus actual data. A simple status report might show performance information, such as percent complete or status dashboards for:**

A. Each area (i.e., scope, schedule, cost, and quality).

B. Recognition and rewards for achieving the project's major milestones.

C. Performance appraisals of project team members.

D. Exceptional performance by individual team members (or sub-teams).

171. **Communication activities have many potential dimensions that generally include all of the following EXCEPT:**

A. Written, oral, and non-verbal.

B. Internal and external.

C. Conceptual and definitive.

D. Formal and informal.

172. **All of the following are information management and distribution tools EXCEPT:**

A. Hard-copy document management.

B. Electronic communications management.

C. Inputting project performance data into a spreadsheet or database.

D. Electronic project management tools.

173. **The total number of potential communication channels for a project with _n_ = 12 stakeholders is:**

   A. $n(n-1)/2$.

   B. $2n/(n-1)$.

   C. $2(n-1)/n$.

   D. 47 potential communications channels.

174. **Lessons learned documentation generally includes all of the following EXCEPT:**

   A. The causes of issues.

   B. Updates of the statement of work to reflect training and learning requirements.

   C. Reasoning behind the corrective action chosen.

   D. Other types of lessons learned about communications management.

175. Techniques and considerations for effective communications management generally includes all of the following EXCEPT:

A. Meeting management techniques, such as preparing an agenda and dealing with conflicts.

B. Facilitation techniques for building consensus and overcoming obstacles.

C. Listening techniques, such as listening actively and removal of barriers that adversely affect comprehension.

D. Providing comfortable chairs in project conference rooms to strengthen project team cohesion.

176. Control Communications is the process of:

A. Ensuring that information is provided on a need-to-know basis only to avoid unnecessary confusion and possible conflicts.

B. Monitoring and controlling communications throughout the entire project life cycle to ensure the information needs of the project stakeholders are met.

C. Providing all project information to all project stakeholders to enhance full buy-in regarding project requirements.

D. Securing and guarding any negative information related to project performance throughout the entire project life cycle to ensure that the project team can continue working on the project with minimal disruption.

Project Risk Management
(Chapter 11 of the *PMBOK® Guide*)

177. The major processes of Project Risk Management are:

A. Plan Risk Management, Identify Risks, Assess Risks, Mitigate Risks, Transfer Risks, and Document outcomes.

B. Identify Risks, Plan Risk Management, Evaluate Risks, Develop Risk Responses, Mitigate Risks, and Document results.

C. Identify Risks, Perform Qualitative Risk Validation, Perform Quantitative Impact Assessment, Develop Risk Response Strategies, Document Response Strategies, and Monitor Risk Responses.

D. Plan Risk Management, Identify Risks, Perform Qualitative Risk Analysis, Perform Quantitative Risk Analysis, Plan Risk Responses, and Control Risks.

178. To be successful, an organization should be committed to addressing risk management:

A. Just in time before a meeting with major stakeholders of the project.

B. Proactively and consistently throughout the project.

C. As soon as time and cost estimates are ready.

D. As early as possible in the execution phase.

179. **Strategies typically used to deal with threats or risks that may have negative impacts on project objectives if they occur include all of the following EXCEPT:**

   A. Interpret.

   B. Avoid.

   C. Transfer.

   D. Mitigate.

180. **Risk transference nearly always involves:**

   A. Eliminating risk through beta testing.

   B. Policies and procedures for a response system.

   C. Accepting a lower profit if some activities overrun their budget.

   D. Payment of a risk premium to the party taking on the risk.

181. **In the Plan Risk Responses process, an accept strategy for a negative risk or threat indicates that the project team has decided:**

A. To agree with the project manager.

B. To eliminate a specific risk or threat, to reduce the probability and/or impact of an adverse risk event to be within acceptable threshold limits, or to pursue an opportunity actively.

C. Not to change the project management plan to deal with a risk, or is unable to identify any other suitable response strategy.

D. To purchase insurance, or to require performance bonds, warranties, and guarantees.

182. **The primary output of the Identify Risks process is the:**

A. Risk register.

B. Expected monetary value of the risk events.

C. List of corrective actions.

D. Risk mitigation plan.

183. **A thorough analysis of the _____ will help identify potential risks to the project.**

    A. Risk identification checklist based on historical information and knowledge.

    B. Project's change control system.

    C. Project's mission statement.

    D. Project's schedule and budget.

184. **All of the following are inputs to the Identify Risks process EXCEPT:**

    A. Risk management plan.

    B. Scope baseline.

    C. Workaround plan.

    D. Quality management plan.

185. **Outputs from the Plan Risk Responses process include all of the following EXCEPT:**

    A. Risk register updates.

    B. Corrective actions.

    C. Project documents updates.

    D. Project management plan updates.

186. Tools and techniques of the Perform Quantitative Risk Analysis process are:

A. Contracting, contingency planning, alternative strategies, and insurance.

B. Interviewing, historical results, workarounds, and response development.

C. Checklists, damage control reports, standard allowances, and inspection.

D. Data gathering and representation techniques, quantitative risk analysis and modeling techniques, and expert judgment.

187. As an output of the Perform Quantitative Risk Analysis process, the risk register is updated. These updates generally include:

A. Prioritized list of quantified risks.

B. Qualitative analysis of the threats to ignore and opportunities to accept.

C. Checklists, corrective actions, and qualified decision trees.

D. Direction, resources, and contingency costs.

188. **Risk impact assessment to investigate the potential effect on a project objective such as schedule, cost, quality, or performance has the following characteristics EXCEPT:**

A. Evaluation of each risk can be conducted using a probability and impact matrix that leads to rating the risks as low, moderate, or high priority.

B. Approaches used in evaluating risk impacts related to project objectives could be relative, numerical, or nonlinear.

C. Usually, risk-rating rules are specified by the organization in advance of the project and can be tailored to the specific project

D. The impact on project objectives should be assessed primarily at the end of the project, as part of the lessons learned.

189. **The outputs from the Control Risks process include all of the following EXCEPT:**

A. Project documents updates.

B. Work breakdown structure (WBS).

C. Change requests.

D. Project management plan updates.

190. The Delphi technique has all of the following characteristics EXCEPT:

A. It is a way to reach a consensus of experts on a subject such as project risk.

B. It is a technique in which project risk experts participate anonymously.

C. It helps reduce bias in the data and keeps any one person from having undue influence on the outcome.

D. It is based on an ancient Greek technique to ensure that actions of subordinates are aligned with the vision of senior executives.

191. The risk rating:

A. Is calculated by multiplying the probability of the occurrence of a risk times its impact (numerical scale) on an objective (e.g., cost, time, scope, or quality) if it were to occur.

B. Is the sum of squares of the scale values assigned to the estimates of probability and impact.

C. Cannot be used to determine whether a risk is considered low, moderate, or high.

D. Is a commonly used technique for risk avoidance.

192. Sensitivity analysis:

A. Examines the extent to which the uncertainty of project objectives affects each project element simultaneously.

B. Examines the extent to which the uncertainty of each project element affects the objective being studied when all other uncertain elements are held at their baseline values.

C. Is a method for assessing stakeholders' tolerance to risk.

D. Cannot be used to determine which risks have the most potential impact on the project.

193. All of the following are characteristics of a decision tree EXCEPT:

A. A decision tree is a diagramming and calculation technique for evaluating the implications of a chain of multiple options in the presence of uncertainty.

B. Decision tree analysis is a risk analysis tool, which can be used to choose the most appropriate responses.

C. A decision tree is primarily a graphical, qualitative risk analysis technique and is not generally used in quantitative risk analysis.

D. Decision tree analysis uses the expected monetary value (EMV) analysis to calculate the average outcome when the future includes scenarios that may or may not happen.

194. **The risk management plan generally includes all of the following EXCEPT:**

    A. Methodology.

    B. Definitions of risk probability and impact.

    C. Responses to individual risks.

    D. Probability and impact matrix.

195. **The Perform Qualitative Risk Analysis process assesses the priority of identified risks using all of the following EXCEPT:**

    A. Relative probability or likelihood of occurrence of identified risks.

    B. Impact on project objectives if the identified risks occur.

    C. A mathematical technique, such as the expected monetary value (EMV), to create the impression of precision and accuracy.

    D. The organization's risk tolerance associated with the project constraints of cost, schedule, scope, and quality.

196. **As an output of the Control Risks process, an updated risk register generally includes some or all of the following EXCEPT:**

A. The work breakdown structure (WBS).

B. Outcomes of risk reassessments, risk audits, and periodic risk reviews.

C. Identification of new risks, updates to probability, impact, priority, response plans, ownership, and other elements of the risk register.

D. Actual outcomes of the project's risks and of the risk responses.

197. **Expected monetary value (EMV) analysis has all of the following characteristics EXCEPT:**

A. It is a statistical concept that calculates the average outcome when the future includes scenarios that may or may not happen.

B. The EMV of opportunities are generally expressed as positive values, whereas those of threats are expressed as negative values.

C. EMV analysis cannot be used effectively in decision tree analysis unless a risk-averse assumption is made.

D. EMV for a project is calculated by multiplying the value of each possible outcome by its probability of occurrence and adding the products together.

198. SWOT Analysis has all of the following characteristics EXCEPT:

A. It is a technique that examines the project from each of the strengths, weaknesses, opportunities, and threats (SWOT) perspectives to increase the breadth of identified risks by including internally generated risks.

B. It identifies strengths and weaknesses of the organization, regardless of the specific project or the general business area.

C. It identifies any opportunities for the project that arise from organizational strengths, and any threats arising from organizational weaknesses.

D. It examines the degree to which organizational strengths offset threats, as well as identifies opportunities that may serve to overcome weaknesses.

Project Procurement Management
(Chapter 12 of the *PMBOK® Guide*)

199. All of the following are inputs to the Plan Procurements process EXCEPT:

A. Risk register.

B. Stakeholder register.

C. Application area extensions.

D. Enterprise environmental factors.

200. Generally, a bid differs from a proposal in that the term:

A. Bid is used when the seller selection decision will be based on price.

B. Bid is used when technical capability or technical approach are paramount.

C. Proposal is used when the selection decision will be based on price.

D. Proposal is used when the project time frame is limited.

201. **The buyer structures procurement documents to accomplish all of the following EXCEPT:**

   A. Facilitate an accurate and complete response from each prospective seller.

   B. Include a description of the desired form of the response.

   C. Include the relevant procurement statement of work (SOW) and any required contractual provisions.

   D. Provide a list of potential bidders to each prospective seller.

202. **Approved change requests can generally include all of the following EXCEPT:**

   A. Modifications to the terms and conditions of the contract.

   B. Modification to pricing.

   C. Seller invoices.

   D. Modification to descriptions of the products, services, or results to be provided.

203. Which of the following is false about advertising as one of the tools and techniques of the Conduct Procurements process?

A. Some government jurisdictions require public advertising of certain types of procurement items.

B. Advertisements in general circulation publications and using online resources can cause public pressure, resulting in bid disputes.

C. Advertising can often be used to expand existing lists of potential sellers.

D. Advertisements can be placed in general circulation publications such as selected newspapers or in specialty trade publications.

204. Payment systems generally include all of the following characteristics EXCEPT:

A. Payments are typically processed after certification of satisfactory work by an authorized person on the project team.

B. All payments should be made and documented in strict accordance with the terms of the contract.

C. Re-negotiations of the price and other terms of the contract are typically conducted prior to authorizing payments to the seller.

D. Payments to the seller are typically processed by the accounts payable system of the buyer.

205. **The buyer, usually through its authorized procurement administrator, provides the seller with _____ as an output of the output of the Close Procurements process.**

A. Formal written notice that the contract has been completed.

B. Letters of commendation to all project team members.

C. Informal notice of acceptance of the deliverables.

D. A copy of the internal notice of completion provided to senior management.

206. **In which type of contracts do buyers need to precisely specify the product or services being procured?**

A. Cost plus award fee contracts.

B. Fixed-price contracts.

C. Cost-reimbursable contracts.

D. Partnership contracts.

207. Which of the following is one of the terms used to describe contested changes and potential constructive changes where the buyer and seller cannot reach an agreement on compensation for the change or cannot agree that a change has occurred?

A. Forcing.

B. Mediation.

C. Complaints.

D. Claims.

208. Constructive changes are:

A. Postponed as long as possible to protect the budget.

B. Viewed as negative, quantified, and tabulated.

C. Uniquely identified and documented by project correspondence.

D. Submitted for bids to the relevant vendor list.

209. The procurement audit has all of the following characteristics EXCEPT:

A. It maintains a complete file of procurement-related records.

B. It is a structured review of the procurement process.

C. It is a review of the procurement process originating from the Plan Procurement Management process through Control Procurements.

D. Its objective is to identify successes and failures that warrant recognition in the preparation or administration of other procurement contracts on the project, or on other projects.

210. All legal contractual relationships generally fall into one of the following broad categories EXCEPT:

A. Request for proposal (RFP).

B. Fixed-price contracts.

C. Cost-reimbursable contracts.

D. Time and material contracts (T&M).

211. All of the following are true about the statement of work (SOW) for a procurement EXCEPT:

A. It describes the procurement item in sufficient detail to allow prospective sellers to determine if they are capable of providing the products, services, or results.

B. It should be as ambiguous, incomplete, and wordy as possible to allow for future negotiations.

C. It can include specifications, quantity desired, quality levels, performance data, period of performance, work location, and other requirements.

D. It can be revised and refined as required as it moves through the procurement process until incorporated into a signed agreement.

212. Outputs from the Close Procurements process generally include all of the following EXCEPT:

A. Closed procurements.

B. Deliverable acceptance.

C. The contractor's working proposal.

D. Lessons learned documentation.

213. **Source selection criteria are developed and used to rate or score seller proposals. These criteria have generally all of the following characteristics EXCEPT:**

A. They are often included as a part of the procurement documents.

B. They can be objective or subjective.

C. They may be limited to only the purchase price if the procurement item is readily available from a number of acceptable sellers.

D. They generally require specification of the name of the transportation organization responsible for delivery of procured products.

214. **All of the following are tools and techniques of the Conduct Procurements process EXCEPT:**

A. Proposal evaluation techniques.

B. Independent estimates.

C. Procurement negotiations.

D. Resource distribution system.

215. Cost plus fixed fee contracts (CPFF) have all of the following characteristics EXCEPT:

A. Seller is reimbursed for all allowable costs for performing the contract work.

B. Seller receives a fixed-fee payment calculated as a percentage of the actual project costs.

C. Seller receives a fixed-fee payment calculated as a percentage of the initial estimated project costs.

D. The fee is paid only for completed work and does not change due to seller performance unless the project scope changes.

216. All of the following are true about the make-or-buy analysis EXCEPT:

A. It should consider all related direct costs but should not consider indirect support costs.

B. Budget constraints may influence make-or-buy decisions. If a buy decision is to be made, then a further decision of whether to purchase or lease is also made.

C. A make-or-buy analysis is a technique used to determine whether particular work can best be accomplished by the project team or should be purchased from outside sources.

D. Available contract types are considered during the buy analysis. The risk sharing between the buyer and seller determines the suitable contract types.

Stakeholder Management
(Chapter 13 of the *PMBOK® Guide*)

217. Stakeholders are:

A. The project engineers who design and construct the project.

B. The people, groups, or organizations that could impact or be impacted by a decision, activity, or outcome of the project.

C. The organization's corporate attorneys.

D. The individuals or agencies that control contingency funds and their disbursement through the project management office (PMO).

218. Which of the following is NOT true about project stakeholders?

A. They are people, groups, or organizations that are actively supportive of the project.

B. They are people, groups, or organizations who are involved in the project.

C. They people, groups, or organizations whose interests may be positively or negatively affected by a decision, activity, or outcome of the project.

D. They are people, groups, or organizations that may exert varying levels of influence over the project and its expected outcomes.

219. To increase the chances to achieve project success, the project manager should do all of the following EXCEPT:

A. Identify the stakeholders early in the project or phase.

B. Analyze the stakeholders levels of interest and individual expectations as well as their importance and influence.

C. As much as possible, create conflicts among various stakeholders to allow the project team to get its work done.

D. Communicate and work with stakeholders to meet their needs/expectations.

220. You are developing management strategies to effectively engage stakeholders throughout the project life cycle, based on the analysis of their needs, interests, and potential impact on project success. This is known as:

A. Manage stakeholder engagement.

B. Control stakeholder engagement.

C. Plan stakeholder management.

D. Manipulate stakeholders.

221. **You are involved in the process of communicating and working with stakeholders to meet their needs/ expectations, address issues as they occur, and foster appropriate stakeholder engagement in project activities throughout the project life cycle. This is known as:**

   A. Manage stakeholder engagement.

   B. Control stakeholder engagement.

   C. Communicate with stakeholders.

   D. Plan stakeholder management.

222. **You are monitoring overall project stakeholder relationships and adjusting strategies and plans for engaging stakeholders. This is known as:**

   A. Manage stakeholder engagement.

   B. Manage stakeholder relationships.

   C. Stakeholders relationship management.

   D. Control stakeholder engagement.

223. **You are using a classification model for stakeholders analysis that groups the stakeholders based on their level of authority and their level or concern regarding the project outcomes. This is known as:**

A. Power/influence grid.

B. Influence/impact grid.

C. Power/interest grid.

D. Salience model.

224. **In developing a stakeholder register, you need to include all of the following EXCEPT:**

A. Identification information.

B. Assessment information.

C. Stakeholder classification.

D. Project risk information.

225. **Classification of the engagement level of stakeholders includes all of the following EXCEPT:**

A. Resistant.

B. Neutral.

C. Supportive.

D. Manipulative.

226. Manage Stakeholder Engagement involves all of the following activities EXCEPT:

A. Clarifying and resolving issues that have been identified.

B. Avoiding potential concerns that have not yet become issues.

C. Anticipating future problems that may be raised by stakeholders.

D. Managing stakeholder expectations through negotiation and communication.

227. All of the following statements about Manage Stakeholder Engagement are true EXCEPT:

A. Managing stakeholder engagement helps to increase the probability of project success.

B. The ability of stakeholders to influence the project is typically highest during the initial stages and gets progressively lower as the project progresses.

C. The ability of stakeholders to influence the project is typically lowest during the initial stages and gets progressively higher as the project progresses.

D. The project manager is responsible for engaging and managing the various stakeholders in a project and may call upon the project sponsor to assist as needed.

228. Control Stakeholder Engagement tools and techniques include all of the following EXCEPT:

A. Information management systems.

B. Expert judgment.

C. Meetings.

D. Behavior modification analytics.

229. Status review meetings are used to:

A. Exchange and analyze information about stakeholder engagement.

B. Manage closely low-power/low-interest stakeholders.

C. Avoid confrontation with high-power/low-interest stakeholders.

D. Update the critical path on a factual basis regardless of stakeholders expectations.

230. The power/interest grid classification model for stakeholders analysis suggests:

A. Keep informed high-power/high-interest stakeholders.

B. Keep satisfied high-power/low-interest stakeholders.

C. Monitor low-power/high-interest stakeholders.

D. Manage closely low-power/low-interest stakeholders.

231. **During a public hearing regarding your company's proposed state-of-the-art water tower, a highly interested resident of the area challenges you: "Would you have this thing built in your own backyard?" Your best answer can proceed with:**

A. Given that you are not listed in the stakeholders' register, I cannot take your concerns seriously.

B. I am sorry that you appear to dislike having this water tower as your neighbor. We will look for another location for it.

C. Given that the experts provided ample information that the proposed location is the most suitable, I would be pleased to have this state-of-the-art water tower as a neighbor.

D. If you want to have usable water pressure in your residence, you should not interfere with our work.

Appendix X3

(Interpersonal Skills)

232. **All of the following are generally true about leadership in a project environment EXCEPT:**

A. It involves focusing the efforts of a group of people toward a common goal and enabling them to work as a team.

B. It is the ability to get things done through others.

C. Respect and trust, rather than fear and submission, are the key elements of effective leadership.

D. Although important throughout all project phases, effective leadership is critical during the Closing phase of a project when the emphasis is on stakeholder acceptance of the project.

233. Team building has all of the following characteristics EXCEPT:

A. It is the process of helping a group of individuals, bound by a common purpose, to work with each other, the leader, external stakeholders, and the organization.

B. It requires handling project team problems decisively and removing the individual(s) responsible for these problems from the team promptly to ensure a productive, smooth project environment.

C. It can be enhanced by obtaining top management support, encouraging team member commitment, introducing appropriate rewards, recognition, and ethics.

D. It can be enhanced by creating a team identity, managing conflicts effectively, promoting trust and open communication among team members, and providing leadership.

234. Motivating in a project environment involves creating an environment to meet project objectives while providing maximum satisfaction related to what people value most. These values generally include all of the following EXCEPT:

A. A sense of accomplishment, achievement, and growth.

B. Sufficient financial compensation.

C. Accurate criticism in the annual performance review or after the project is completed.

D. Opportunity to apply one's professional skills to meet new challenges.

235. **Project managers spend the majority of their time communicating with team members and other project stakeholders. To communicate effectively, the project manager should generally do all of the following EXCEPT:**

A. Calculate the potential number of communication channels accurately and update it regularly to develop a bridge between diverse stakeholders and a common perspective on the project among them, regardless of their cultural and organizational backgrounds.

B. Develop an awareness of the communication styles of other parties, cultural nuances/norms, relationships, personalities, and the overall context of the situation.

C. Identify various communication channels, understand what information they need to provide, what information they need to receive, and which interpersonal skills will help them communicate effectively with various project stakeholders.

D. Use active and passive listening techniques to gain insight to problem areas, negotiation and conflict management strategies, decision making, and problem resolution.

236. Cultural differences:

A. Are primarily individual issues that need to be avoided in project teams.

B. Involve internal stakeholders primarily and should not be apparent to external stakeholders because such differences do not involve them.

C. Can impact the speed of working, the decision-making process, and the impulse to act without appropriate planning.

D. Should not generally lead to conflict and stress in organizations. Therefore, they do not affect the performance of professionals working on project teams and their ability to meet project objectives.

Glossary

237. Acceptance Criteria:

A. Are developed during phase-end reviews to ensure authorization to close the current phase and start the subsequent one.

B. Are a set of conditions that are required to be met before deliverables are accepted.

C. Can be passive or active allowing the project team to deal with the risks as they occur.

D. Are distinct from performance measurements, which are aimed at meeting or exceeding technical specifications.

238. A code of accounts:

A. Is a numbering system used to uniquely identify each component of the work breakdown structure (WBS).

B. Includes work packages, used to track phase completion.

C. Is an organizational scheme to keep track of contracts.

D. Charts elements of the WBS against the timeline.

239. The cost baseline is the approved:

A. Project schedule and is used as a basis for comparison with actual results.

B. Description of the project scope specified in the project charter.

C. Version of the time-phased project budget, excluding any management reserves, which can be changed only through formal change control procedures.

D. Starting point for contract negotiations.

240. The scope management plan for a project is:

A. The project specifications which include project objectives, design principles, and guidance on how the project will be controlled.

B. A three-level project work breakdown structure that shows how project scope will be managed.

C. The document that shows that all project deliverables were completed satisfactorily.

D. A component of the project or program management plan that describes how the scope will be defined, developed, monitored, controlled, and verified.

241. The project scope statement:

A. Is a description of the project scope, major deliverables, assumptions, and constraints.

B. Determines the boundary conditions and responses required to perform project activities.

C. Is a narrative analysis of project activities, activity sequences, activity durations, and resource requirements.

D. Is a written statement that identifies the quality standards relevant to project deliverables and describes how to achieve those standards.

242. A work package is:

A. A summary task or a hammock activity at the top level of the work breakdown structure (WBS).

B. The work defined at the lowest level of the work breakdown structure for which cost and duration can be estimated and managed.

C. A management control point that may include one or more control accounts to plan a project deliverable and establish integrated schedule change control.

D. A milestone required for completion of a project deliverable in the work breakdown structure (WBS) or a work activity on the critical path.

243. In what way does free float differ from total float?

A. Free float is the amount of total float that does not affect the schedule end date or violate a schedule constraint, whereas total float is the total accumulated amount of free float.

B. There is no difference—the two terms are functionally equivalent and are used in different application areas.

C. Free float is the amount of time that a schedule activity can be delayed without delaying the early start date of any successor or violating a schedule constraint, whereas total float is the amount of time that a schedule activity can be delayed or extended from its early start date without delaying the project finish date or violating a schedule constraint.

D. Free float of a schedule activity is calculated by subtracting the total float of the schedule activity from the total float of the critical path, without violating other schedule constraints.

244. The project's performance measurement baseline:

A. Is used to measure and manage performance.

B. Changes frequently.

C. Documents relevant performance standards of the project team.

D. Can be generally changed by the project team to reflect adherence to project objectives.

245. What does cost of quality mean?

A. The sacrifice of unessential project objectives to meet essential quality standards.

B. The life cycle cost of the project, including costs for quality planning and failure costs.

C. Determining the costs of meeting project objectives, including costs for quality control, quality assurance, and rework.

D. Determining the costs incurred to ensure quality.

246. FFP is an acronym for:

A. Free-Flow Performance Management.

B. Firm-Fixed-Price Contract.

C. Free-Form Project.

D. Fixed-File Procurement.

247. The approved project baseline may only be changed:

A. When a sequence of activities has taken longer than originally planned or costs more than originally estimated, and in excess of the thresholds established in the performance management plan.

B. When a change request is generated and approved through the Perform Integrated Change Control process.

C. When the productivity within a certain discipline has been substantially higher or lower than originally planned, and in excess of the thresholds established in the performance measurement plan.

D. When a high-duration activity has been accomplished "out-of-sequence."

248. All of the following are true about the product life cycle EXCEPT:

A. It is a series of phases that represent the evolution of a product.

B. The last product life cycle phase for a product is generally the product's retirement.

C. Operations are ongoing endeavors that produce repetitive outputs according to the standards institutionalized in a product life cycle.

D. The project life cycle contains one or more product life cycles, and therefore the two life cycles are synonymous.

249. **The iterative process of increasing the level of detail in a project management plan as greater amounts of information and more accurate estimates become available is called:**

A. Quality function deployment (QFD).

B. Agile project planning method.

C. Progressive elaboration.

D. Sequential planning method (SPM).

250. **Workaround is:**

A. A response to a threat that has occurred, for which a prior response had not been planned or was not effective.

B. A contingency plan to avoid, transfer, or mitigate a negative risk or threat.

C. Implementation of the established contingency plan to avoid a negative risk or threat, or to exploit a positive risk or an opportunity.

D. Using global sourcing to continue project work around the clock.

Q & As
FOR THE
PMBOK® GUIDE
FIFTH EDITION
Answers

Introduction
(Chapter 1 of the *PMBOK® Guide*)

1. Answer: D.
PMBOK® Guide, page 3, Section 1.2

What is a project?
A project is a temporary endeavor undertaken to create a unique product, service, or result.

2. Answer: B.
PMBOK® Guide, page 5, Section 1.3

What is project management?
Project management is the application of knowledge, skills, tools, and techniques to project activities to meet project requirements.

3. Answer: A.
PMBOK® Guide, page 6, Section 1.3

Managing a project typically includes, but is not limited to:
- Identifying requirements;
- Addressing the various needs, concerns, and expectations of the stakeholders in planning and executing the project;
- Setting up, maintaining, and carrying out communications among stakeholders that are active, effective, and collaborative in nature;
- Managing stakeholders towards meeting project requirements and creating project deliverables;
- Balancing the competing project constraints, which include, but are not limited to:
  - Scope,
  - Quality,
  - Schedule,
  - Budget,
  - Resources, and
  - Risks.

The specific project characteristics and circumstances can influence the constraints on which the project management team needs to focus.

4. Answer: C.
PMBOK® Guide, page 10, Section 1.4.2

Portfolio Management
…
Portfolio management refers to the centralized management of one or more portfolios to achieve strategic objectives. Portfolio management focuses on ensuring that projects and programs are reviewed to prioritize resource allocation, and that the management of the portfolio is consistent with and aligned to organizational strategies.

5. Answer: A.

PMBOK® Guide, page 8, Section 1.4, Table 1-1

Comparative Overview of Project, Program, and Portfolio Management

As shown in Table 1-1, under the heading *Projects*:

Success is measured by product and project quality, timeliness, budget compliance, and degree of customer satisfaction.

6. Answer: B.

PMBOK® Guide, page 9, Section 1.4.1

Program Management

A program is defined as a group of related projects, subprograms, and program activities managed in a coordinated way to obtain benefits not available from managing them individually. Programs may include elements of related work outside the scope of the discrete projects in the program. A project may or may not be part of a program but a program will always have projects.

7. Answer: C.

PMBOK® Guide, pages 10–11, Section 1.4.4

There are several types of PMO structures in organizations, each varying in the degree of control and influence they have on projects within the organization, such as:

- **Supportive.** Supportive PMOs provide a consultative role to projects by supplying templates, best practices, training, access to information and lessons learned from other projects. This type of PMO serves as a project repository. The degree of control provided by the PMO is low.
- **Controlling.** Controlling PMOs provide support and require compliance through various means. Compliance may involve adopting project management frameworks or methodologies, using specific templates, forms and tools, or conformance to governance. The degree of control provided by the PMO is moderate.
- **Directive.** Directive PMOs take control of the projects by directly managing the projects. The degree of control provided by the PMO is high.

8. Answer: A.

PMBOK® Guide, page 11, Section 1.4.4

Project Management Office

…

A primary function of a PMO is to support project managers in a variety of ways which may include, but are not limited to:

- Managing shared resources across all projects administered by the PMO;
- Identifying and developing project management methodology, best practices, and standards;
- Coaching, mentoring, training, and oversight;
- Monitoring compliance with project management standards, policies, procedures, and templates by means of project audits;
- Developing and managing project policies, procedures, templates, and other shared documentation (organizational process assets); and
- Coordinating communication across projects.

9. Answer: D.

PMBOK® Guide, pages 12–13, Sections 1.5 and 1.5.1

Relationship Between Project Management, Operations Management, and Organizational Strategy

Operations management is responsible for overseeing, directing, and controlling business operations. Operations evolve to support the day-to-day business, and are necessary to achieve strategic and tactical goals of the business. Examples include: production operations, manufacturing operations, accounting operations, software support, and maintenance.

Though temporary in nature, projects can help achieve the organizational goals when they are aligned with the organization's strategy. Organizations sometimes change their operations, products, or systems by creating strategic business initiatives that are developed and implemented through projects. Projects require project management activities and skill sets, while operations require business process management, operations management activities, and skill sets.

Operations and Project Management

Changes in business operations may be the focus of a dedicated project—especially if there are substantial changes to business operations as a result of a new product or service delivery. Ongoing operations are outside of the scope of a project; however, there are intersecting points where the two areas cross.

Projects can intersect with operations at various points during the product life cycle, such as:

- At each closeout phase;
- When developing a new product, upgrading a product, or expanding outputs;
- While improving operations or the product development process; or
- Until the end of the product life cycle.

At each point, deliverables and knowledge are transferred between the project and operations for implementation of the delivered work. This implementation occurs through a transfer of project resources to operations toward the end of the project, or through a transfer of operational resources to the project at the start.

Operations are ongoing endeavors that produce repetitive outputs, with resources assigned to do basically the same set of tasks according to the standards institutionalized in a product life cycle. Unlike the ongoing nature of operations, projects are temporary endeavors.

10. Answer: D.

PMBOK® Guide, page 16, Section 1.6

Business Value

...

Portfolio management aligns components (projects, programs, or operations) to the organizational strategy, organized into portfolios or subportfolios to optimize project or program objectives, dependencies, costs, timelines, benefits, resources, and risks. This allows organizations to have an overall view of how the strategic goals are reflected in the portfolio, institute appropriate governance management, and authorize human, financial, or material resources to be allocated based on expected performance and benefits.

11. Answer: B.

PMBOK® Guide, page 17, Section 1.71

Responsibilities and Competencies of the Project Manager

In general, project managers have the responsibility to satisfy the needs: task needs, team needs, and individual needs. As project management is a critical strategic discipline, the project manager becomes the link between the strategy and the team. Projects are essential to the growth and survival of organizations. Projects create value in the form of improved business processes, are indispensable in the development of new products and services, and make it easier for companies to respond to changes in the environment, competition, and the marketplace. The project manager's role therefore becomes increasingly strategic. However, understanding and applying the knowledge, tools, and techniques that are recognized as good practice are not sufficient for effective project management. In addition to any area-specific skills and general management proficiencies required for the project, effective project management requires that the project manager possess the following competencies:

- **Knowledge**—Refers to what the project manager knows about project management.
- **Performance**—Refers to what the project manager is able to do or accomplish while applying his or her project management knowledge.
- **Personal**—Refers to how the project manager behaves when performing the project or related activity. Personal effectiveness encompasses attitudes, core personality characteristics, and leadership, which provides the ability to guide the project team while achieving project objectives and balancing the project constraints.

12. Answer: C.

PMBOK® Guide, page 18, Section 1.8

Project Management Body of Knowledge

The *PMBOK® Guide* contains the standard for managing most projects most of the time across many types of industries. The standard, included in Annex A1, describes the project management processes used to manage a project toward a more successful outcome.

This standard is unique to the project management field and has interrelationships to other project management disciplines such as program management and portfolio management.

Project management standards do not address all details of every topic. This standard is limited to individual projects and the project management processes that are generally recognized as good practice. Other standards may be consulted for additional information on the broader context in which projects are accomplished, such as:

- *The Standard for Program Management* [3] addresses the management of programs,
- *The Standard for Portfolio Management* [4] addresses the management of portfolios,
- *Organizational Project Management Maturity Model (OPM3®)* [5] examines an enterprise's project management process capabilities.

Project Life Cycle and Organization
(Chapter 2 of the *PMBOK® Guide*)

13. Answer: D.
PMBOK® Guide, page 20, Section 2.1.1

Organizational Cultures and Styles
… Cultures and styles are learned and shared and may have a strong influence on a project's ability to meet its objectives. A project manager should therefore understand the different organizational styles and cultures that may affect a project. The project manager needs to know which individuals in the organization are the decision makers or influencers and work with them to increase the probability of project success.

In light of globalization, understanding the impact of cultural influences is critical in projects involving diverse organizations and locations around the world. Culture becomes a critical factor in defining project success, and multi-cultural competence becomes critical for the project manager

14. Answer: C.
PMBOK® Guide, pages 21–22, Section 2.1.3 and Table 2-1, page 25, and Figure 2-5

Organizational Structure
At the opposite end of the spectrum to the functional organization is the projectized organization, shown in Figure 2-5. In a projectized organization, team members are often colocated. Most of the organization's resources are involved in project work, and project managers have a great deal of independence and authority. Virtual collaboration techniques are often used to accomplish the benefits of colocated teams. Projectized organizations often have organizational units called departments, but they can either report directly to the project manager or provide support services to the various projects.

15. Answer: A.
PMBOK® Guide, pages 21–22, Section 2.1.3 Table 2-1, and Figure 2-1

Organizational Structure
Organizational structure is an enterprise environmental factor, which can affect the availability of resources and influence how projects are conducted (see also Section 2.1.5). Organizational structures range from functional to projectized, with a variety of matrix structures in between. Table 2-1 shows key project-related characteristics of the major types of organizational structures.

The classic functional organization, shown in Figure 2-1, is a hierarchy where each employee has one clear superior. Staff members are grouped by specialty, such as production, marketing, engineering, and accounting at the top level. Specialties may be further subdivided into focused functional units, such as mechanical and electrical engineering. Each department in a functional organization will do its project work independently of other departments.

16. Answer: C.
PMBOK® Guide, page 23, Section 2.1.3 and Figure 2-2

Organizational Structure
Matrix organizations, as shown in Figures 2-2 through 2-4, reflect a blend of functional and projectized characteristics. Matrix organizations can be classified as weak, balanced, or strong depending on the relative level of power and influence between functional and project managers. Weak matrix organizations maintain many of the characteristics of a functional organization, and the role of the project manager is more of a coordinator or expediter. A project expediter works as staff assistant and communications coordinator. The expediter cannot personally make or enforce decisions. Project coordinators have power to make some decisions, have some authority, and report to a higher-level manager.

17. Answer: C.
PMBOK® Guide, pages 21–22, Section 2.1.3, and Table 2-1

Organizational Structure
Organizational structure is an enterprise environmental factor, which can affect the availability of resources and influence how projects are conducted (see also Section 2.1.5). Organizational structures range from functional to projectized, with a variety of matrix structures in between. Table 2-1 shows key project-related characteristics of the major types of organizational structures.

18. Answer: A.
PMBOK® Guide, pages 21–22, Section 2.1.3, Table 2-1, page 25, and Figure 2-5

Organizational Structure
Organizational structure is an enterprise environmental factor, which can affect the availability of resources and influence how projects are conducted (see also Section 2.1.5). Organizational structures range from functional to projectized, with a variety of matrix structures in between. Table 2-1 shows key project-related characteristics of the major types of organizational structures.

…

At the opposite end of the spectrum to the functional organization is the projectized organization, shown in Figure 2-5. In a projectized organization, team members are often colocated. Most of the organization's resources are involved in project work, and project managers have a great deal of independence and authority. Virtual collaboration techniques are often used to accomplish the benefits of colocated teams. Projectized organizations often have organizational units called departments, but they can either report directly to the project manager or provide support services to the various projects.

19. Answer: B.
PMBOK® Guide, page 23, Section 2.1.3, Table 2-1, and Figure 2-4

Organizational Structure
Strong matrix organizations have many of the characteristics of the projectized organization, and have full-time project managers with considerable authority and full-time project administrative staff. While the balanced matrix organization recognizes the need for a project manager, it does not provide the project manager with the full authority over the project and project funding. Table 2-1 provides additional details of the various matrix organizational structures.

20. Answer: D.
PMBOK® Guide, page 23, Section 2.1.3, Table 2-1, and Figures 2-2 through 2-4

Organizational Structure
Matrix organizations, as shown in Figures 2-2 through 2-4, reflect a blend of functional and projectized characteristics. Matrix organizations can be classified as weak, balanced, or strong depending on the relative level of power and influence between functional and project managers. Weak matrix organizations maintain many of the characteristics of a functional organization, and the role of the project manager is more of a coordinator or expediter. A project expediter works as staff assistant and communications coordinator. The expediter cannot personally make or enforce decisions. Project coordinators have power to make some decisions, have some authority, and report to a higher-level manager. Strong matrix organizations have many of the characteristics of the projectized organization, and have full-time project managers with considerable authority and full-time project administrative staff. While the balanced matrix organization recognizes the need for a project manager, it does not provide the project manager with the full authority over the project and project funding. Table 2-1 provides additional details of the various matrix organizational structures.

21. Answer: D.

PMBOK® Guide, page 29, Section 2.1.5

Enterprise Environmental Factors

Enterprise environmental factors refer to conditions, not under the control of the project team, that influence, constrain, or direct the project. Enterprise environmental factors are considered inputs to most planning processes, may enhance or constrain project management options, and may have a positive or negative influence on the outcome.

Enterprise environmental factors vary widely in type or nature. Enterprise environmental factors include, but are not limited to:

- Organizational culture, structure, and governance;
- Geographic distribution of facilities and resources;
- Government or industry standards (e.g., regulatory agency regulations, codes of conduct, product standards, quality standards, and workmanship standards);
- Infrastructure (e.g., existing facilities and capital equipment);
- Existing human resources (e.g., skills, disciplines, and knowledge, such as design, development, legal, contracting, and purchasing);
- Personnel administration (e.g., staffing and retention guidelines, employee performance reviews and training records, reward and overtime policy, and time tracking);
- Company work authorization systems;
- Marketplace conditions;
- Stakeholder risk tolerances;
- Political climate;
- Organization's established communications channels;
- Commercial databases (e.g., standardized cost estimating data, industry risk study information, and risk databases); and
- Project management information system (e.g., an automated tool, such as a scheduling software tool, a configuration management system, an information collection and distribution system, or web interfaces to other online automated systems).

22. Answer: B.

PMBOK® Guide, page 33, Section 2.2

Project Stakeholders

…

Functional managers. Functional managers are key individuals who play a management role within an administrative or functional area of the business, such as human resources, finance, accounting, or procurement. They are assigned their own permanent staff to carry out the ongoing work, and they have a clear directive to manage all tasks within their functional area of responsibility. The functional manager may provide subject matter expertise or their function may provide services to the project.

23. Answer: C.

PMBOK® Guide, page 32, Section 2.2.1

Project Stakeholders

…

An important part of a project manager's responsibility is to manage stakeholder expectations, which can be difficult because stakeholders often have very different or conflicting objectives. Part of the project manager's responsibility is to balance these interests and ensure that the project team interacts with stakeholders in a professional and cooperative manner. Project managers may involve the project's sponsor or other team members from different locations to identify and manage stakeholders that could be dispersed around the world.

24. **Answer: B.**

PMBOK® Guide, page 34, Section 2.2.2

Project Governance

Project governance is an oversight function that is aligned with the organization's governance model and that encompasses the project life cycle. Project governance framework provides the project manager and team with structure, processes, decision-making models and tools for managing the project, while supporting and controlling the project for successful delivery. Project governance is a critical element of any project, especially on complex and risky projects. It provides a comprehensive, consistent method of controlling the project and ensuring its success by defining and documenting and communicating reliable, repeatable project practices. It includes a framework for making project decisions; defines roles, responsibilities, and accountabilities for the success of the project; and determines the effectiveness of the project manager. A project's governance is defined by and fits within the larger context of the portfolio, program, or organization sponsoring it but is separate from organizational governance.

For project governance, the PMO may also play some decisive role. Project governance involves stakeholders as well as documented policies, procedures, and standards; responsibilities; and authorities.

25. Answer: B.
PMBOK® Guide, page 38, Section 2.4

Project Life Cycle
A project life cycle is the series of phases that a project passes through from its initiation to its closure. The phases are generally sequential, and their names and numbers are determined by the management and control needs of the organization or organizations involved in the project, the nature of the project itself, and its area of application. The phases can be broken down by functional or partial objectives, intermediate results or deliverables, specific milestones within the overall scope of work, or financial availability. Phases are generally time bounded, with a start and ending or control point. A life cycle can be documented within a methodology. The project life cycle can be determined or shaped by the unique aspects of the organization, industry, or technology employed. While every project has a definite start and a definite end, the specific deliverables and activities that take place in between will vary widely with the project. The life cycle provides the basic framework for managing the project, regardless of the specific work involved.

26. Answer: D.

PMBOK® Guide, pages 38–41, Section 2.4.1, Figure 2-8, and Figure 2-9

Characteristics of the Project Life Cycle

…

The generic life cycle structure generally displays the following characteristics:

- Cost and staffing levels are low at the start, peak as the work is carried out, and drop rapidly as the project draws to a close. Figure 2-8 illustrates this typical pattern.
- The typical cost and staffing curve above may not apply to all projects. A project may require significant expenditures to secure needed resources early in its life cycle, for instance, or be fully staffed from a point very early in its life cycle.
- Risk and uncertainty (as illustrated in Figure 2-9) are greatest at the start of the project. These factors decrease over the life of the project as decisions are reached and as deliverables are accepted.
- The ability to influence the final characteristics of the project's product, without significantly impacting cost, is highest at the start of the project and decreases as the project progresses towards completion. Figure 2-9 illustrates the idea that the cost of making changes and correcting errors typically increases substantially as the project approaches completion.

27. Answer: D.

PMBOK® Guide, pages 44–45, Section 2.4.2.2, Figure 2-13, Section 2.4.2.3, and Glossary

Predictive Life Cycles

Predictive life cycles (also known as fully plan-driven) are ones in which the project scope, and the time and cost required to deliver that scope, are determined as early in the project life cycle as practically possible. As shown in Figure 2-13, these projects proceed through a series of sequential or overlapping phases, with each phase generally focusing on a subset of project activities and project management processes. The work performed in each phase is usually different in nature to that in the preceding and subsequent phases, therefore, the makeup and skills required of the project team may vary from phase to phase.

Iterative and Incremental Life Cycles

Iterative and incremental life cycles are ones in which project phases (also called iterations) intentionally repeat one or more project activities as the project team's understanding of the product increases. Iterations develop the product through a series of repeated cycles, while increments successively add to the functionality of the product. These life cycles develop the product both iteratively and incrementally.

Product life cycle. The series of phases that represent the evolution of a product, from concept through delivery, growth, maturity, and to retirement.

Project life cycle. The series of phases that a project passes through from its initiation to its closure.

28. **Answer: B.**

PMBOK® Guide, pages 44–46, Section 2.4.2.2, Figure 2-13, Section 2.4.2.3, and Section 2.4.2.4

Predictive Life Cycles

Predictive life cycles (also known as fully plan-driven) are ones in which the project scope, and the time and cost required to deliver that scope, are determined as early in the project life cycle as practically possible. As shown in Figure 2-13, these projects proceed through a series of sequential or overlapping phases, with each phase generally focusing on a subset of project activities and project management processes. The work performed in each phase is usually different in nature to that in the preceding and subsequent phases, therefore, the makeup and skills required of the project team may vary from phase to phase.

Iterative and Incremental Life Cycles

Iterative and incremental life cycles are ones in which project phases (also called iterations) intentionally repeat one or more project activities as the project team's understanding of the product increases. Iterations develop the product through a series of repeated cycles, while increments successively add to the functionality of the product. These life cycles develop the product both iteratively and incrementally.

Adaptive Life Cycles

Adaptive life cycles (also known as change-driven or agile methods) are intended to respond to high levels of change and ongoing stakeholder involvement. Adaptive methods are also iterative and incremental, but differ in that iterations are very rapid (usually with a duration of 2 to 4 weeks) and are fixed in time and cost. Adaptive projects generally perform several processes in each iteration, although early iterations may concentrate more on planning activities

Project Management Processes

(Chapter 3 of the *PMBOK® Guide*)

29. Answer: B.

PMBOK® Guide, pages 48–49, Introduction

Project management processes are grouped into
five categories known as Project Management Process
Groups (or Process Groups):

- **Initiating Process Group.** Those processes
  performed to define a new project or a new phase of
  an existing project by obtaining authorization to start
  the project or phase.
- **Planning Process Group.** Those processes required
  to establish the scope of the project, refine the
  objectives, and define the course of action required to
  attain the objectives that the project was undertaken to
  achieve.
- **Executing Process Group.** Those processes
  performed to complete the work defined in the project
  management plan to satisfy the project specifications.
- **Monitoring and Controlling Process Group.** Those
  processes required to track, review, and regulate the
  progress and performance of the project; identify any
  areas in which changes to the plan are required; and
  initiate the corresponding changes.
- **Closing Process Group.** Those processes performed
  to finalize all activities across all Process Groups to
  formally close the project or phase.

30. Answer: A.

PMBOK® Guide, page 51, Section 3.1 and Figure 3-2

Common Project Management Process Interactions
Project Management Process Groups are linked by
the outputs which are produced. The Process Groups
are seldom either discrete or one-time events; they
are overlapping activities that occur throughout the
project. The output of one process generally becomes
an input to another process or is a deliverable of the
project, subproject, or project phase. Deliverables at the
subproject or project level may be called incremental
deliverables. The Planning Process Group provides the
Executing Process Group with the project management
plan and project documents, and, as the project
progresses, it often creates updates to the project
management plan and the project documents. Figure 3-2
illustrates how the Process Groups interact and shows
the level of overlap at various times. If the project is
divided into phases, the Process Groups interact within
each phase.

31. Answer: C.

PMBOK® Guide, page 51, Section 3.1

Common Project Management Process Interactions
Project Management Process Groups are linked by
the outputs which are produced. The Process Groups
are seldom either discrete or one-time events; they
are overlapping activities that occur throughout the
project. The output of one process generally becomes
an input to another process or is a deliverable of the
project, subproject, or project phase. Deliverables at the
subproject or project level may be called incremental
deliverables. The Planning Process Group provides the
Executing Process Group with the project management
plan and project documents, and, as the project
progresses, it often creates updates to the project
management plan and the project documents.

32. Answer: D.

PMBOK® Guide, page 51, Section 3.1 and Figure 3-2; and page 52, Section 3.2

Common Project Management Process Interactions
If the project is divided into phases, the Process Groups interact within each phase.

Project Management Process Groups
The Process Groups are not project life cycle phases. In fact, it is possible that all Process Groups could be conducted within a phase. As projects are separated into distinct phases or subcomponents, such as concept development feasibility study, design, prototype, build, or test, etc., all of the Process Groups would normally be repeated for each phase or subcomponent along the lines explained previously and illustrated in Figure 3-2.

33. Answer: C.

PMBOK® Guide, pages 47–48, Introduction

In order for a project to be successful, the project team should:
- Select appropriate processes required to meet the project objectives;
- Use a defined approach that can be adapted to meet requirements;
- Establish and maintain appropriate communication and engagement with stakeholders;
- Comply with requirements to meet stakeholder needs and expectations; and
- Balance the competing constraints of scope, schedule, budget, quality, resources, and risk to produce the specified product, service, or result.

...

Project management processes apply globally and across industry groups. Good practice means there is general agreement that the application of project management processes has been shown to enhance the chances of success over a wide range of projects. Good practice does not mean that the knowledge, skills, and processes described should always be applied uniformly on all projects. For any given project, the project manager, in collaboration with the project team, is always responsible for determining which processes are appropriate, and the appropriate degree of rigor for each process.

34. Answer: C.

PMBOK® Guide, pages 50–51, Section 3.1, and Figures 3-1 and 3-2

Common Project Management Process Interactions

Project Management Process Groups are linked by the outputs which are produced. The Process Groups are seldom either discrete or one-time events; they are overlapping activities that occur throughout the project. The output of one process generally becomes an input to another process or is a deliverable of the project, subproject, or project phase. Deliverables at the subproject or project level may be called incremental deliverables. The Planning Process Group provides the Executing Process Group with the project management plan and project documents, and, as the project progresses, it often creates updates to the project management plan and the project documents. Figure 3-2 illustrates how the Process Groups interact and shows the level of overlap at various times. If the project is divided into phases, the Process Groups interact within each phase.

When a project is divided into phases, the Process Groups are used, as appropriate, to effectively drive the project to completion in a controlled manner. In multiphase projects, processes are repeated within each phase until the criteria for phase completion have been satisfied.

35. Answer: A.
PMBOK® Guide, page 54, Section 3.3 and Figure 3-4

Initiating Process Group
The Initiating Process Group consists of those processes performed to define a new project or a new phase of an existing project by obtaining authorization to start the project or phase. Within the Initiating processes, the initial scope is defined and initial financial resources are committed. Internal and external stakeholders who will interact and influence the overall outcome of the project are identified. If not already assigned, the project manager will be selected. This information is captured in the project charter and stakeholder register. When the project charter is approved, the project becomes officially authorized. Although the project management team may help write the project charter, this standard assumes that business case assessment, approval, and funding are handled externally to the project boundaries (Figure 3-4).

36. Answer: B.
PMBOK® Guide, page 54, Section 3.3

Initiating Process Group
…
Performing the Initiating processes at the start of each phase helps to keep the project focused on the business need that the project was undertaken to address. The success criteria are verified, and the influence, drivers and objectives of the project stakeholders are reviewed. A decision is then made as to whether the project should be continued, delayed, or discontinued.

Involving the sponsors, customers, and other stakeholders during initiation creates a shared understanding of success criteria, reduces the overhead of involvement, and generally improves deliverable acceptance, customer satisfaction, and other stakeholder satisfaction.

37. Answer: B.
PMBOK® Guide, page 55, Section 3.4; page 61, Table 3-1; and page 227, Introduction

Planning Process Group
The Planning Process Group consists of those processes performed to establish the total scope of the effort, define and refine the objectives, and develop the course of action required to attain those objectives. The Planning processes develop the project management plan and the project documents that will be used to carry out the project.

...

Table 3-1 reflects the mapping of the 47 project management processes within the 5 Project Management Process Groups and the 10 Knowledge Areas.

Plan Quality Management—The process of identifying quality requirements and/or standards for the project and its deliverables and documenting how the project will demonstrate compliance with quality requirements.

38. Answer: B.
PMBOK® Guide, page 57, Section 3.6; page 61, Table 3-1; and page 141, Introduction

Monitoring and Controlling Process Group
The Monitoring and Controlling Process Group consists of those processes required to track, review, and orchestrate the progress and performance of the project; identify any areas in which changes to the plan are required; and initiate the corresponding changes.

Control Schedule—The process of monitoring the status of project activities to update project progress and manage changes to the schedule baseline to achieve the plan.

39. Answer: D.
PMBOK® Guide, page 56, Section 3.5; page 57, Section 3.7; and page 61, Table 3-1

Executing Process Group
The Executing Process Group consists of those processes performed to complete the work defined in the project management plan to satisfy the project specifications. This Process Group involves coordinating people and resources, managing stakeholder expectations, as well as integrating and performing the activities of the project in accordance with the project management plan.

Closing Process Group
The Closing Process Group consists of those processes performed to conclude all activities across all Project Management Process Groups to formally complete the project, phase, or contractual obligations. This Process Group, when completed, verifies that the defined processes are completed within all of the Process Groups to close the project or a project phase, as appropriate, and formally establishes that the project or project phase is complete.

40. Answer: A.
PMBOK® Guide, page 60, Section 3.9; and page 61, Table 3-1

Role of the Knowledge Areas
The 47 project management processes identified in the *PMBOK® Guide* are further grouped into ten separate Knowledge Areas. A Knowledge Area represents a complete set of concepts, terms, and activities that make up a professional field, project management field, or area of specialization. These ten Knowledge Areas are used on most projects most of the time. Project teams should utilize these ten Knowledge Areas and other knowledge areas, as appropriate, for their specific project.
…

Table 3-1 reflects the mapping of the 47 project management processes within the 5 Project Management Process Groups and the 10 Knowledge Areas.

Project Integration Management
(Chapter 4 of the *PMBOK® Guide*)

41. Answer: A.
PMBOK® Guide, page 63, Introduction; and page 65, Figure 4-1

Project Integration Management
Project Integration Management includes the processes and activities to identify, define, combine, unify, and coordinate the various processes and project management activities within the Project Management Process Groups. In the project management context, integration includes characteristics of unification, consolidation, communication, and integrative actions that are crucial to controlled project execution through completion, successfully managing stakeholder expectations, and meeting requirements. Project Integration Management includes making choices about resource allocation, making trade-offs among competing objectives and alternatives, and managing the interdependencies among the project management Knowledge Areas. The project management processes are usually presented as discrete processes with defined interfaces while, in practice, they overlap and interact in ways that cannot be completely detailed in the *PMBOK® Guide*.

Figure 4-1 provides an overview of the Project Integration Management processes, which are as follows:

4.1 Develop Project Charter—The process of developing a document that formally authorizes the existence of a project and provides the project manager with the authority to apply organizational resources to project activities.

4.2 Develop Project Management Plan—The process of defining, preparing, and coordinating all subsidiary plans and integrating them into a comprehensive project management plan. The project's integrated baselines and subsidiary plans may be included within the project management plan.

4.3 Direct and Manage Project Work—The process of leading and performing the work defined in the project management plan and implementing approved changes to achieve the project's objectives.

4.4 Monitor and Control Project Work—The process of tracking, reviewing, and reporting project progress against the performance objectives defined in the project management plan.

4.5 Perform Integrated Change Control—The process of reviewing all change requests; approving changes and managing changes to deliverables, organizational process assets, project documents, and the project management plan; and communicating their disposition.

4.6 Close Project or Phase—The process of finalizing all activities across all of the Project Management Process Groups to formally complete the phase or project.

42. Answer: C.
PMBOK® Guide, pages 66–68, Section 4.1

Develop Project Charter

Develop Project Charter is the process of developing a document that formally authorizes the existence of a project and provides the project manager with the authority to apply organizational resources to project activities. The key benefit of this process is a well-defined project start and project boundaries, creation of a formal record of the project, and a direct way for senior management to formally accept and commit to the project...

The project charter establishes a partnership between the performing and requesting organizations. In the case of external projects, a formal contract is typically the preferred way to establish an agreement. In this case, the project team becomes the seller responding to conditions of an offer to buy from an outside entity. A project charter is still used to establish internal agreements within an organization to assure proper delivery under the contract. The approved project charter formally initiates the project. A project manager is identified and assigned as early in the project as is feasible, preferably while the project charter is being developed and always prior to the start of planning. The project charter should be authored by the sponsoring entity. The project charter provides the project manager with the authority to plan and execute the project. It is recommended that the project manager participate in the development of the project charter to obtain a foundational understanding of the project requirements. This understanding will better allow for efficient resources allocation to project activities.

Projects are initiated by an entity external to the project such as a sponsor, program or project management office (PMO) staff person, or a portfolio governing body chairperson or authorized representative. The project initiator or sponsor should be at the level that is appropriate to procure funding and commit resources to the project. Projects are initiated due to internal business needs or external influences. These needs or influences often trigger the creation of a needs analysis, feasibility study, business case, or description of the situation that the project will address. Chartering a project validates alignment of the project to the strategy and ongoing work of the organization. A project charter is not considered to be a contract, because there is no consideration or money promised or exchanged in its creation.

43. Answer: D.
PMBOK® Guide, pages 83–84, Section 4.3.2 and Section 4.3.2.2

Direct and Manage Project Work: Tools and Techniques
…

Project Management Information System
The project management information system, which is part of the environmental factors, provides access to tools, such as a scheduling tool, a work authorization system, a configuration management system, an information collection and distribution system, or interfaces to other online automated systems. Automated gathering and reporting on key performance indicators (KPI) can be part of this system.

44. Answer: D.
PMBOK® Guide, pages 98–99, Section 4.5.2; and page 100, Figure 4-12

Perform Integrated Change Control: Tools and Techniques
.1 Expert Judgment
In addition to the project management team's expert judgment, stakeholders may be asked to provide their expertise and may be asked to sit on the change control board (CCB). Such judgment and expertise are applied to any technical and management details during this process and may be provided by various sources…
.2 Meetings
In this case, these meetings are usually referred to as change control meetings. When needed for the project, a change control board (CCB) is responsible for meeting and reviewing the change requests and approving, rejecting, or other disposition of those changes…

45. Answer: A.
PMBOK® Guide, pages 94–96, Section 4.5

Perform Integrated Change Control
Perform Integrated Change Control is the process of reviewing all change requests; approving changes and managing changes to deliverables, organizational process assets, project documents, and the project management plan; and communicating their disposition. It reviews all requests for changes or modifications to project documents, deliverables, baselines, or the project management plan and approves or rejects the changes. The key benefit of this process is that it allows for documented changes within the project to be considered in an integrated fashion while reducing project risk, which often arises from changes made without consideration to the overall project objectives or plans…

The Perform Integrated Change Control process is conducted from project inception through completion and is the ultimate responsibility of the project manager. The project management plan, the project scope statement, and other deliverables are maintained by carefully and continuously managing changes, either by rejecting changes or by approving changes, thereby assuring that only approved changes are incorporated into a revised baseline.

46. Answer: B.
PMBOK® Guide, page 96, Section 4.5

Perform Integrated Change Control
Configuration control is focused on the specification of both the deliverables and the processes; while change control is focused on identifying, documenting, and approving or rejecting changes to the project documents, deliverables, or baselines.

47. Answer: C.

PMBOK® Guide, page 94, Section 4.5; and Glossary

Perform Integrated Change Control

Every documented change request needs to be either approved or rejected by a responsible individual, usually the project sponsor or project manager. The responsible individual will be identified in the project management plan or by organizational procedures. When required, the Perform Integrated Change Control process includes a change control board (CCB), which is a formally chartered group responsible for reviewing, evaluating, approving, delaying, or rejecting changes to the project, and for recording and communicating such decisions. Approved change requests can require new or revised cost estimates, activity sequences, schedule dates, resource requirements, and analysis of risk response alternatives. These changes can require adjustments to the project management plan and other project documents. The applied level of change control is dependent upon the application area, complexity of the specific project, contract requirements, and the context and environment in which the project is performed. Customer or sponsor approval may be required for certain change requests after CCB approval, unless they are part of the CCB.

Change Control Board (CCB). A formally chartered group responsible for reviewing, evaluating, approving, delaying, or rejecting changes to the project, and for recording and communicating such decisions.

48. Answer: B.
PMBOK® Guide, pages 96–97, Section 4.5

Perform Integrated Change Control
Some of the configuration management activities included in the Perform Integrated Change Control process are as follows:

- **Configuration identification.** Identification and selection of a configuration item to provide the basis for which the product configuration is defined and verified, products and documents are labeled, changes are managed, and accountability is maintained.
- **Configuration status accounting.** Information is recorded and reported as to when appropriate data about the configuration item should be provided. This information includes a listing of approved configuration identification, status of proposed changes to the configuration, and the implementation status of approved changes.
- **Configuration verification and audit.** Configuration verification and configuration audits ensure the composition of a project's configuration items is correct and that corresponding changes are registered, assessed, approved, tracked, and correctly implemented. This ensures the functional requirements defined in the configuration documentation have been met.

49. Answer: A.
PMBOK® Guide, pages 100–101, Section 4.6

Close Project or Phase
Close Project or Phase is the process of finalizing all activities across all of the Project Management Process Groups to formally complete the project or phase...

This includes all planned activities necessary for administrative closure of the project or phase, including step-by-step methodologies that address:
- Actions and activities necessary to satisfy completion or exit criteria for the phase or project;
- Actions and activities necessary to transfer the project's products, services, or results to the next phase or to production and/or operations; and
- Activities needed to collect project or phase records, audit project success or failure, gather lessons learned and archive project information for future use by the organization.

50. Answer: D.
PMBOK® Guide, pages 92–94, Section 4.4.3; and pages 103–104, Section 4.6.3

Monitor and Control Project Work: Outputs
.1 Change Requests
.2 Work Performance Reports
.3 Project Management Plan Updates
.4 Project Documents Updates

Close Project or Phase: Outputs
.1 Final Product, Service, or Result Transition
.2 Organizational Process Assets Updates

Project Scope Management
(Chapter 5 of the *PMBOK® Guide*)

51. Answer: D.
PMBOK® Guide, pages 109–110, Section 5.1.3.1; and page 138, Section 5.6.1.1

Scope Management Plan
The scope management plan is a component of the project or program management plan that describes how the scope will be defined, developed, monitored, controlled, and verified. The scope management plan is a major input into the Develop Project Management Plan process, and the other scope management processes…

The scope management plan can be formal or informal, broadly framed or highly detailed, based on the needs of the project.

Project Management Plan
Described in Section 4.2.3.1. The following information from the project management plan is used to control scope:
- **Scope baseline.** The scope baseline is compared to actual results to determine if a change, corrective action, or preventive action is necessary.
- **Scope management plan.** Sections from the scope management plan describe how the project scope will be monitored and controlled.
  …

52. Answer: C.

PMBOK® Guide, pages 110–112, Section 5.2

Collect Requirements

Collect Requirements is the process of determining, documenting, and managing stakeholder needs and requirements to meet project objectives. The key benefit of this process is that it provides the basis for defining and managing the project scope including product scope...

The project's success is directly influenced by active stakeholder involvement in the discovery and decomposition of needs into requirements and by the care taken in determining, documenting, and managing the requirements of the product, service, or result of the project. Requirements include conditions or capabilities that are to be met by the project or present in the product, service, or result to satisfy an agreement or other formally imposed specification. Requirements include the quantified and documented needs and expectations of the sponsor, customer, and other stakeholders. These requirements need to be elicited, analyzed, and recorded in enough detail to be included in the scope baseline and to be measured once project execution begins. Requirements become the foundation of the WBS. Cost, schedule, quality planning, and sometimes procurement are all based upon these requirements. The development of requirements begins with an analysis of the information contained in the project charter (Section 4.1.3.1), the stakeholder register (Section 13.1.3.1), and the stakeholder management plan (Section 13.2.3.1).

53. Answer: D.

PMBOK® Guide, page 113, Section 5.2.1.5; and page 398, Section 13.1.3.1

Collect Requirements: Inputs
...

Stakeholder Register
... The stakeholder register is used to identify stakeholders who can provide information on the requirements. The stakeholder register also captures major requirements and main expectations stakeholders may have for the project.

Stakeholder Register
The main output of the Identify Stakeholders process is the stakeholder register. This contains all details related to the identified stakeholders including, but not limited to:
- **Identification information.** Name, organizational position, location, role in the project, contact information;
- **Assessment information.** Major requirements, main expectations, potential influence in the project, phase in the life cycle with the most interest; and
- **Stakeholder classification.** Internal/external, supporter/neutral/resistor, etc.

54. Answer: D.

PMBOK® Guide, pages 118–119, Section 5.2.3.2 and Figure 5-6

Requirements Traceability Matrix
The requirements traceability matrix is a grid that links product requirements from their origin to the deliverables that satisfy them. The implementation of a requirements traceability matrix helps ensure that each requirement adds business value by linking it to the business and project objectives. It provides a means to track requirements throughout the project life cycle, helping to ensure that requirements approved in the requirements documentation are delivered at the end of the project. Finally, it provides a structure for managing changes to the product scope.

55. Answer: C.
PMBOK® Guide, page 120, Figure 5-7; and pages 123–125, Section 5.3.3

Define Scope: Outputs
.1 Project Scope Statement
.2 Project Documents Updates

56. Answer: A.
PMBOK® Guide, page 123, Section 5.3.3.1

Project Scope Statement
The project scope statement is the description of the project scope, major deliverables, assumptions, and constraints. The project scope statement documents the entire scope, including project and product scope. It describes, in detail, the project's deliverables and the work required to create those deliverables. It also provides a common understanding of the project scope among project stakeholders. It may contain explicit scope exclusions that can assist in managing stakeholder expectations. It enables the project team to perform more detailed planning, guides the project team's work during execution, and provides the baseline for evaluating whether requests for changes or additional work are contained within or outside the project's boundaries.

57. Answer: A.
PMBOK® Guide, pages 125–126, Section 5.4

Create WBS
Create WBS is the process of subdividing project deliverables and project work into smaller, more manageable components. The key benefit of this process is that it provides a structured vision of what has to be delivered...

The WBS is a hierarchical decomposition of the total scope of work to be carried out by the project team to accomplish the project objectives and create the required deliverables. The WBS organizes and defines the total scope of the project, and represents the work specified in the current approved project scope statement.

The planned work is contained within the lowest level of WBS components, which are called work packages. A work package can be used to group the activities where work is scheduled and estimated, monitored, and controlled. In the context of the WBS, work refers to work products or deliverables that are the result of activity and not to the activity itself.

58. Answer: A.
PMBOK® Guide, page 124, Section 5.3.3.1

Project Scope Statement
Constraints. A limiting factor that affects the execution of a project or process. Constraints identified with the project scope statement list and describe the specific internal or external restrictions or limitations associated with the project scope that affect the execution of the project, for example, a predefined budget or any imposed dates or schedule milestones that are issued by the customer or performing organization. When a project is performed under an agreement, contractual provisions will generally be constraints. Information on constraints may be listed in the project scope statement or in a separate log.

59. Answer: B.
PMBOK® Guide, page 120, Figure 5-7; and pages 121–122, Section 5.3.1

Define Scope: Inputs
.1 Scope Management Plan
.2 Project Charter
.3 Requirements Documentation
.4 Organizational Process Assets

60. Answer: A.
PMBOK® Guide, pages 125–126, Section 5.4

Create WBS
Create WBS is the process of subdividing project deliverables and project work into smaller, more manageable components. The key benefit of this process is that it provides a structured vision of what has to be delivered…

The WBS is a hierarchical decomposition of the total scope of work to be carried out by the project team to accomplish the project objectives and create the required deliverables. The WBS organizes and defines the total scope of the project, and represents the work specified in the current approved project scope statement.

61. Answer: B.
PMBOK® Guide, page 132, Section 5.4.3.1

Scope Baseline
WBS. The WBS is a hierarchical decomposition of the total scope of work to be carried out by the project team to accomplish the project objectives and create the required deliverables. Each descending level of the WBS represents an increasingly detailed definition of the project work. The WBS is finalized by assigning each work package to a control account and establishing a unique identifier for that work package from a code of accounts.

62. Answer: A.
PMBOK® Guide, pages 133–134, Section 5.5

Validate Scope
Validate Scope is the process of formalizing acceptance of the completed project deliverables. The key benefit of this process is that it brings objectivity to the acceptance process and increases the chance of final product, service, or result acceptance by validating each deliverable…

The Validate Scope process differs from the Control Quality process in that the former is primarily concerned with acceptance of the deliverables, while quality control is primarily concerned with correctness of the deliverables and meeting the quality requirements specified for the deliverables. Control Quality is generally performed before Validate Scope, although the two processes may be performed in parallel.

63. Answer: B.

PMBOK® Guide, page 132, Section 5.4.3.1

Scope Baseline

...

- **WBS dictionary.** The WBS dictionary is a document that provides detailed deliverable, activity, and scheduling information about each component in the WBS. The WBS dictionary is a document that supports the WBS.

64. Answer: D.

PMBOK® Guide, page 133, Figure 5-14; page 136, Figure 5-16; pages 135–136, Section 5.5.3; and pages 139–140, Section 5.6.3

Control Scope: Outputs
.1 Work Performance Information
.2 Change Requests
.3 Project Management Plan Updates
.4 Project Documents Updates
.5 Organizational Process Assets Updates

Validate Scope: Outputs
.1 Accepted Deliverables
.2 Change Requests
.3 Work Performance Information
.4 Project Documents Updates

65. Answer: C.

PMBOK® Guide, pages 136–137, Section 5.6; and page 139, Section 5.6.2.1

Control Scope

Control Scope is the process of monitoring the status of the project and product scope and managing changes to the scope baseline. The key benefit of this process is that it allows the scope baseline to be maintained throughout the project…

Controlling the project scope ensures all requested changes and recommended corrective or preventive actions are processed through the Perform Integrated Change Control process (see Section 4.5). Control Scope is also used to manage the actual changes when they occur and is integrated with the other control processes. The uncontrolled expansion to product or project scope without adjustments to time, cost, and resources is referred to as scope creep. Change is inevitable; therefore some type of change control process is mandatory for every project.

Variance Analysis

Variance analysis is a technique for determining the cause and degree of difference between the baseline and actual performance. Project performance measurements are used to assess the magnitude of variation from the original scope baseline. Important aspects of project scope control include determining the cause and degree of variance relative to the scope baseline (Section 5.4.3.1) and deciding whether corrective or preventive action is required.

Project Time Management
(Chapter 6 of the *PMBOK® Guide*)

66. Answer: B.
PMBOK® Guide, page 141, Introduction; and page 143, Figure 6-1

Project Time Management
Project Time Management includes the processes required to manage the timely completion of the project.

Figure 6-1 provides an overview of the Project Time Management processes, which are as follows:

6.1 Plan Schedule Management—The process of establishing the policies, procedures, and documentation for planning, developing, managing, executing, and controlling the project schedule.

6.2 Define Activities—The process of identifying and documenting the specific actions to be performed to produce the project deliverables.

6.3 Sequence Activities—The process of identifying and documenting relationships among the project activities.

6.4 Estimate Activity Resources—The process of estimating the type and quantities of material, human resources, equipment, or supplies required to perform each activity.

6.5 Estimate Activity Durations—The process of estimating the number of work periods needed to complete individual activities with estimated resources.

6.6 Develop Schedule—The process of analyzing activity sequences, durations, resource requirements, and schedule constraints to create the project schedule model.

6.7 Control Schedule—The process of monitoring the status of project activities to update project progress and manage changes to the schedule baseline to achieve the plan.

67. Answer: B.

PMBOK® Guide, page 152, Section 6.2.2.2

Rolling Wave Planning

Rolling wave planning is an iterative planning technique in which the work to be accomplished in the near term is planned in detail, while the work in the future is planned at a higher level. It is a form of progressive elaboration. Therefore, work can exist at various levels of detail depending on where it is in the project life cycle. During early strategic planning, when information is less defined, work packages may be decomposed to the known level of detail. As more is known about the upcoming events in the near term, work packages can be decomposed into activities.

68. Answer: A.

PMBOK® Guide, page 156, Section 6.3.2.1

Precedence Diagramming Method

The precedence diagramming method (PDM) is a technique used for constructing a schedule model in which activities are represented by nodes and are graphically linked by one or more logical relationships to show the sequence in which the activities are to be performed. Activity-on-node (AON) is one method of representing a precedence diagram. This is the method used by most project management software packages.

69. Answer: D.

PMBOK® Guide, page 165, Section 6.4.3.1; and page 167, Section 6.5.1.4

Activity Resource Requirements

Activity resource requirements identify the types and quantities of resources required for each activity in a work package. These requirements then can be aggregated to determine the estimated resources for each work package and each work period. The amount of detail and the level of specificity of the resource requirement descriptions can vary by application area. The resource requirements documentation for each activity can include the basis of estimate for each resource, as well as the assumptions that were made in determining which types of resources are applied, their availability, and what quantities are used.

Activity Resource Requirements

Described in Section 6.4.3.1. The estimated activity resource requirements will have an effect on the duration of the activity, since the level to which the resources assigned to the activity meet the requirements will significantly influence the duration of most activities. For example, if additional or lower-skilled resources are assigned to an activity, there may be reduced efficiency or productivity due to increased communication, training, and coordination needs leading to a longer duration estimate.

70. Answer: A.

PMBOK® Guide, page 181, Section 6.6.2.7

Schedule Compression

Schedule compression techniques are used to shorten the schedule duration without reducing the project scope, in order to meet schedule constraints, imposed dates, or other schedule objectives. Schedule compression techniques include, but are not limited to:

- **Crashing.** A technique used to shorten the schedule duration for the least incremental cost by adding resources. Examples of crashing include approving overtime, bringing in additional resources, or paying to expedite delivery to activities on the critical path. Crashing works only for activities on the critical path where additional resources will shorten the activity's duration. Crashing does not always produce a viable alternative and may result in increased risk and/or cost.

…

71. Answer: B.

PMBOK® Guide, page 181, Section 6.6.2.7

Schedule Compression

Schedule compression techniques are used to shorten the schedule duration without reducing the project scope, in order to meet schedule constraints, imposed dates, or other schedule objectives. Schedule compression techniques include, but are not limited to:

…

- **Fast tracking.** A schedule compression technique in which activities or phases normally done in sequence are performed in parallel for at least a portion of their duration. An example is constructing the foundation for a building before completing all of the architectural drawings. Fast tracking may result in rework and increased risk. Fast tracking only works if activities can be overlapped to shorten the project duration.

72. Answer: C.

PMBOK® Guide, pages 157–158, Section 6.3.2.2

Dependency Determination

Dependencies may be characterized by the following attributes: mandatory or discretionary, internal or external, as described below. Dependency has four attributes, but two can be applicable at the same time in following ways: mandatory external dependencies, mandatory internal dependencies, discretionary external dependencies, or discretionary internal dependencies.

- **Mandatory dependencies.** Mandatory dependencies are those that are legally or contractually required or inherent in the nature of the work. Mandatory dependencies often involve physical limitations, such as on a construction project, where it is impossible to erect the superstructure until after the foundation has been built, or on an electronics project, where a prototype has to be built before it can be tested. Mandatory dependencies are also sometimes referred to as hard logic or hard dependencies. Technical dependencies may not be mandatory. The project team determines which dependencies are mandatory during the process of sequencing the activities. Mandatory dependencies should not be confused with assigning schedule constraints in the scheduling tool.

- **Discretionary dependencies.** Discretionary dependencies are sometimes referred to as preferred logic, preferential logic, or soft logic. Discretionary dependencies are established based on knowledge of best practices within a particular application area or some unusual aspect of the project where a specific sequence is desired, even though there may be other acceptable sequences. Discretionary dependencies should be fully documented since they can create arbitrary total float values and can limit later scheduling options. When fast tracking techniques are employed, these discretionary dependencies should be reviewed and considered for modification or removal. The project team determines which dependencies are discretionary during the process of sequencing the activities.

...

73. Answer: D.
PMBOK® Guide, pages 149–151, Figure 6-5 and Section 6.2.1

Define Activities: Inputs
.1 Schedule Management Plan
.2 Scope Baseline
.3 Enterprise Environmental Factors
.4 Organizational Process Assets

74. Answer: C.
PMBOK® Guide, page 182, Section 6.6.3.2

Project Schedule

…

Bar charts. These charts, also known as Gantt charts, represent schedule information where activities are listed on the vertical axis, dates are shown on the horizontal axis, and activity durations are shown as horizontal bars placed according to start and finish dates. Bar charts are relatively easy to read, and are frequently used in management presentations. For control and management communications, the broader, more comprehensive summary activity, sometimes referred to as a hammock activity, is used between milestones or across multiple interdependent work packages, and is displayed in bar chart reports.

75. Answer: C.
PMBOK® Guide, page 156, Section 6.3.2.1

Precedence Diagramming Method
The precedence diagramming method (PDM) is a technique used for constructing a schedule model in which activities are represented by nodes and are graphically linked by one or more logical relationships to show the sequence in which the activities are to be performed. Activity-on-node (AON) is one method of representing a precedence diagram. This is the method used by most project management software packages.

76. Answer: B.

PMBOK® Guide, pages 176–177, Section 6.6.2.2

Critical Path Method

The critical path method, which is a method used to estimate the minimum project duration and determine the amount of scheduling flexibility on the logical network paths within the schedule model. This schedule network analysis technique calculates the early start, early finish, late start, and late finish dates for all activities without regard for any resource limitations by performing a forward and backward pass analysis through the schedule network, as shown in Figure 6-18. In this example the longest path includes activities A, C, and D, and, therefore, the sequence of A-C-D is the critical path. The critical path is the sequence of activities that represents the longest path through a project, which determines the shortest possible project duration. The resulting early and late start and finish dates are not necessarily the project schedule, rather they indicate the time periods within which the activity could be executed, using the parameters entered in the schedule model for activity durations, logical relationships, leads, lags, and other known constraints. The critical path method is used to calculate the amount of scheduling flexibility on the logical network paths within the schedule model.

On any network path, the schedule flexibility is measured by the amount of time that a schedule activity can be delayed or extended from its early start date without delaying the project finish date or violating a schedule constraint, and is termed "total float." A CPM critical path is normally characterized by zero total float on the critical path. As implemented with PDM sequencing, critical paths may have positive, zero, or negative total float depending on constraints applied...

77. Answer: C.

PMBOK® Guide, pages 179–180, Section 6.6.2.4; and page 189, Section 6.7.2.3

Resource Optimization Techniques

Examples of resource optimization techniques that can be used to adjust the schedule model due to demand and supply of resources include, but are not limited to:

- **Resource leveling.** A technique in which start and finish dates are adjusted based on resource constraints with the goal of balancing demand for resources with the available supply. Resource leveling can be used when shared or critically required resources are only available at certain times, or in limited quantities, or over-allocated, such as when a resource has been assigned to two or more activities during the same time period, as shown in Figure 6-20, or to keep resource usage at a constant level. Resource leveling can often cause the original critical path to change, usually to increase.

- **Resource smoothing.** A technique that adjusts the activities of a schedule model such that the requirements for resources on the project do not exceed certain predefined resource limits. In resource smoothing, as opposed to resource leveling, the project's critical path is not changed and the completion date may not be delayed. In other words, activities may only be delayed within their free and total float. Thus resource smoothing may not be able to optimize all resources.

Resource Optimization Techniques

Described in Section 6.6.2.4. Resource optimization techniques involve the scheduling of activities and the resources required by those activities while taking into consideration both the resource availability and the project time.

78. Answer: A.

PMBOK® Guide, page 178, Section 6.6.2.3

Critical Chain Method

The critical chain method (CCM) is a schedule method that allows the project team to place buffers on any project schedule path to account for limited resources and project uncertainties. It is developed from the critical path method approach and considers the effects of resource allocation, resource optimization, resource leveling, and activity duration uncertainty on the critical path determined using the critical path method. To do so, the critical chain method introduces the concept of buffers and buffer management. The critical chain method uses activities with durations that do not include safety margins, logical relationships, and resource availability with statistically determined buffers composed of the aggregated safety margins of activities at specified points on the project schedule path to account for limited resources and project uncertainties. The resource-constrained critical path is known as the critical chain.

79. Answer: C.

PMBOK® Guide, page 161, Figure 6-12 and pages 162–163, Section 6.4.1

Estimate Activity Resources: Inputs
.1 Schedule Management Plan
.2 Activity List
.3 Activity Attributes
.4 Resource Calendars
.5 Risk Register
.6 Activity Cost Estimates
.7 Enterprise Environmental Factors
.8 Organizational Process Assets

80. Answer: C.

PMBOK® Guide, page 165, Section 6.4.3.1; and page 260, Section 9.1.1.2

Activity Resource Requirements

Activity resource requirements identify the types and quantities of resources required for each activity in a work package. These requirements then can be aggregated to determine the estimated resources for each work package and each work period. The amount of detail and the level of specificity of the resource requirement descriptions can vary by application area. The resource requirements documentation for each activity can include the basis of estimate for each resource, as well as the assumptions that were made in determining which types of resources are applied, their availability, and what quantities are used.

Activity Resource Requirements

Described in Section 6.4.3.1. Human resource planning uses activity resource requirements to determine the human resource needs for the project. The preliminary requirements regarding the required project team members and their competencies are progressively elaborated as part of the Plan Human Resource Management process.

81. Answer: D.

PMBOK® Guide, pages 158–159, Section 6.3.2.3 and
Figure 6-10

Leads and Lags

A lead is the amount of time whereby a successor
activity can be advanced with respect to a predecessor
activity. For example, on a project to construct a new
office building, the landscaping could be scheduled
to start two weeks prior to the scheduled punch list
completion. This would be shown as a finish-to-start
with a two-week lead as shown in Figure 6-10. Lead
is often represented as a negative value for lag in
scheduling software.

A lag is the amount of time whereby a successor activity
will be delayed with respect to a predecessor activity.
For example, a technical writing team may begin
editing the draft of a large document 15 days after they
begin writing it. This can be shown as a start-to-start
relationship with a 15-day lag as shown in Figure 6-10.
Lag can also be represented in project schedule
network diagrams as shown in Figure 6-11 in the
relationship between activities H and I, as indicated by
the nomenclature SS+10 (start-to-start plus 10 days lag)
even though offset is not shown relative to a timescale.

The project management team determines the
dependencies that may require a lead or a lag to
accurately define the logical relationship. The use
of leads and lags should not replace schedule logic.
Activities and their related assumptions should be
documented.

82. Answer: B.

PMBOK® Guide, pages 170–171, Section 6.5.2.4; and Glossary

Three-Point Estimating

The accuracy of single-point activity duration estimates may be improved by considering estimation uncertainty and risk. This concept originated with the program evaluation and review technique (PERT). PERT uses three estimates to define an approximate range for an activity's duration:

- **Most likely** (tM). This estimate is based on the duration of the activity, given the resources likely to be assigned, their productivity, realistic expectations of availability for the activity, dependencies on other participants, and interruptions.
- **Optimistic** (tO). The activity duration based on analysis of the best-case scenario for the activity.
- **Pessimistic** (tP). The activity duration based on analysis of the worst-case scenario for the activity.

Depending on the assumed distribution of values within the range of the three estimates the expected duration, tE, can be calculated using a formula. Two commonly used formulas are triangular and beta distributions...

Program Evaluation and Review Technique (PERT).

A technique for estimating that applies a weighted average of optimistic, pessimistic, and most likely estimates when there is uncertainty with the individual activity estimates.

83. **Answer: A.**
PMBOK® Guide, pages 169–170, Section 6.5.2.2

Analogous Estimating

Analogous estimating is a technique for estimating the duration or cost of an activity or a project using historical data from a similar activity or project. Analogous estimating uses parameters from a previous, similar project, such as duration, budget, size, weight, and complexity, as the basis for estimating the same parameter or measure for a future project. When estimating durations, this technique relies on the actual duration of previous, similar projects as the basis for estimating the duration of the current project. It is a gross value estimating approach, sometimes adjusted for known differences in project complexity. Analogous duration estimating is frequently used to estimate project duration when there is a limited amount of detailed information about the project.

Analogous estimating is generally less costly and less time consuming than other techniques, but it is also less accurate. Analogous duration estimates can be applied to a total project or to segments of a project and may be used in conjunction with other estimating methods. Analogous estimating is most reliable when the previous activities are similar in fact and not just in appearance, and the project team members preparing the estimates have the needed expertise.

84. Answer: D.

PMBOK® Guide, page 178, Section 6.6.2.3 and Figure 6-19

Critical Chain Method

…

The critical chain method adds duration buffers that are non-work schedule activities to manage uncertainty. One buffer, placed at the end of the critical chain, as shown in Figure 6-19, is known as the project buffer and protects the target finish date from slippage along the critical chain. Additional buffers, known as feeding buffers, are placed at each point where a chain of dependent activities that are not on the critical chain feeds into the critical chain. Feeding buffers thus protect the critical chain from slippage along the feeding chains. The size of each buffer should account for the uncertainty in the duration of the chain of dependent activities leading up to that buffer. Once the buffer schedule activities are determined, the planned activities are scheduled to their latest possible planned start and finish dates. Consequently, instead of managing the total float of network paths, the critical chain method focuses on managing the remaining buffer durations against the remaining durations of chains of activities.

85. Answer: C.

PMBOK® Guide, pages 170–171, Section 6.5.2.4

Three-Point Estimating

…

Depending on the assumed distribution of values within the range of the three estimates the expected duration, *tE*, can be calculated using a formula. Two commonly used formulas are triangular and beta distributions. The formulas are:

- **Triangular Distribution.** $tE = (tO + tM + tP) / 3$
- **Beta Distribution** (from the traditional PERT technique). $tE\ 5\ (tO + 4tM + tP) / 6$

Duration estimates based on three points with an assumed distribution provide an expected duration and clarify the range of uncertainty around the expected duration.

86. Answer: B.
PMBOK® Guide, pages 170–171, Section 6.5.2.4

Three-Point Estimating
...
Depending on the assumed distribution of values within the range of the three estimates the expected duration, *tE*, can be calculated using a formula. Two commonly used formulas are triangular and beta distributions. The formulas are:
- **Triangular Distribution.** $tE = (tO + tM + tP) / 3$
- **Beta Distribution** (from the traditional PERT technique). $tE = (tO + 4tM + tP) / 6$

Duration estimates based on three points with an assumed distribution provide an expected duration and clarify the range of uncertainty around the expected duration.

87. Answer: A.
PMBOK® Guide, pages 170–171, Section 6.5.2.4

Three-Point Estimating
...
Depending on the assumed distribution of values within the range of the three estimates the expected duration, *tE*, can be calculated using a formula. Two commonly used formulas are triangular and beta distributions. The formulas are:
- **Triangular Distribution.** $tE = (tO + tM + tP) / 3$
- **Beta Distribution** (from the traditional PERT technique). $tE = (tO \; 1 \; 4tM + tP) / 6$

Duration estimates based on three points with an assumed distribution provide an expected duration and clarify the range of uncertainty around the expected duration.

88. Answer: A.
PMBOK® Guide, pages 176–177, Section 6.6.2.2 and
Figure 6-18

Critical Path Method
The critical path method, which is a method used to
estimate the minimum project duration and determine
the amount of scheduling flexibility on the logical
network paths within the schedule model. This schedule
network analysis technique calculates the early start,
early finish, late start, and late finish dates for all
activities without regard for any resource limitations
by performing a forward and backward pass analysis
through the schedule network, as shown in Figure 6-18.
In this example the longest path includes activities A,
C, and D, and, therefore, the sequence of A-C-D is
the critical path. The critical path is the sequence of
activities that represents the longest path through a
project, which determines the shortest possible project
duration...

On any network path, the schedule flexibility is
measured by the amount of time that a schedule activity
can be delayed or extended from its early start date
without delaying the project finish date or violating a
schedule constraint, and is termed "total float." A CPM
critical path is normally characterized by zero total
float on the critical path. As implemented with PDM
sequencing, critical paths may have positive, zero, or
negative total float depending on constraints applied.
Any activity on the critical path is called a critical
path activity. Positive total float is caused when the
backward pass is calculated from a schedule constraint
that is later than the early finish date that has been
calculated during forward pass calculation. Negative
total float is caused when a constraint on the late dates
is violated by duration and logic. Schedule networks
may have multiple near-critical paths. Many software
packages allow the user to define the parameters
used to determine the critical path(s). Adjustments to
activity durations (if more resources or less scope can
be arranged), logical relationships (if the relationships
were discretionary to begin with), leads and lags, or

other schedule constraints may be necessary to produce network paths with a zero or positive total float. Once the total float for a network path has been calculated, then the free float—the amount of time that a schedule activity can be delayed without delaying the early start date of any successor or violating a schedule constraint—can also be determined. For example the free float for Activity B, in Figure 6-18, is 5 days.

89. Answer: B.

PMBOK® Guide, pages 176–177, Section 6.6.2.2 and
Figure 6-18

Critical Path Method

The critical path method, which is a method used to
estimate the minimum project duration and determine
the amount of scheduling flexibility on the logical
network paths within the schedule model. This schedule
network analysis technique calculates the early start,
early finish, late start, and late finish dates for all
activities without regard for any resource limitations
by performing a forward and backward pass analysis
through the schedule network, as shown in Figure 6-18.
In this example the longest path includes activities A,
C, and D, and, therefore, the sequence of A-C-D is the
critical path. The critical path is the sequence of activities
that represents the longest path through a project, which
determines the shortest possible project duration…

90. Answer: A.

PMBOK® Guide, page 181, Section 6.6.2.7; and Glossary

Schedule Compression

Schedule compression techniques are used to
shorten the schedule duration without reducing the
project scope, in order to meet schedule constraints,
imposed dates, or other schedule objectives. Schedule
compression techniques include, but are not limited to:

- **Crashing.** A technique used to shorten the schedule
  duration for the least incremental cost by adding
  resources. Examples of crashing include approving
  overtime, bringing in additional resources, or paying
  to expedite delivery to activities on the critical path.
  Crashing works only for activities on the critical path
  where additional resources will shorten the activity's
  duration. Crashing does not always produce a viable
  alternative and may result in increased risk and/or cost.
  …

Crashing. A technique used to shorten the schedule
duration for the least incremental cost by adding resources.

91. Answer: B.

PMBOK® Guide, pages 176–177, Section 6.6.2.2 and Figure 6-18

Critical Path Method

The critical path method, which is a method used to estimate the minimum project duration and determine the amount of scheduling flexibility on the logical network paths within the schedule model. This schedule network analysis technique calculates the early start, early finish, late start, and late finish dates for all activities without regard for any resource limitations by performing a forward and backward pass analysis through the schedule network, as shown in Figure 6-18. In this example the longest path includes activities A, C, and D, and, therefore, the sequence of A-C-D is the critical path. The critical path is the sequence of activities that represents the longest path through a project, which determines the shortest possible project duration. The resulting early and late start and finish dates are not necessarily the project schedule, rather they indicate the time periods within which the activity could be executed, using the parameters entered in the schedule model for activity durations, logical relationships, leads, lags, and other known constraints. The critical path method is used to calculate the amount of scheduling flexibility on the logical network paths within the schedule model.

92. Answer: B.

PMBOK® Guide, pages 176–177, Section 6.6.2.2 and Figure 6-18

Critical Path Method

…

On any network path, the schedule flexibility is measured by the amount of time that a schedule activity can be delayed or extended from its early start date without delaying the project finish date or violating a schedule constraint, and is termed "total float." A CPM critical path is normally characterized by zero total float on the critical path. As implemented with PDM sequencing, critical paths may have positive, zero, or negative total float depending on constraints applied. Any activity on the critical path is called a critical path activity. Positive total float is caused when the backward pass is calculated from a schedule constraint that is later than the early finish date that has been calculated during forward pass calculation. Negative total float is caused when a constraint on the late dates is violated by duration and logic. Schedule networks may have multiple near-critical paths. Many software packages allow the user to define the parameters used to determine the critical path(s). Adjustments to activity durations (if more resources or less scope can be arranged), logical relationships (if the relationships were discretionary to begin with), leads and lags, or other schedule constraints may be necessary to produce network paths with a zero or positive total float. Once the total float for a network path has been calculated, then the free float—the amount of time that a schedule activity can be delayed without delaying the early start date of any successor or violating a schedule constraint—can also be determined. For example the free float for Activity B, in Figure 6-18, is 5 days.

Project Cost Management
. (Chapter 7 of the *PMBOK® Guide*)

93. Answer: B.
PMBOK® Guide, page 193, Introduction; and page 194,
Figure 7-1

Project Cost Management
Project Cost Management includes the processes
involved in planning, estimating, budgeting, financing,
funding, managing, and controlling costs so that the
project can be completed within the approved budget.

Figure 7-1 provides an overview of the following Project
Cost Management processes:

7.1 Plan Cost Management—The process
that establishes the policies, procedures, and
documentation for planning, managing, expending,
and controlling project costs.

7.2 Estimate Costs—The process of developing an
approximation of the monetary resources needed to
complete project activities.

7.3 Determine Budget—The process of aggregating
the estimated costs of individual activities or work
packages to establish an authorized cost baseline.

7.4 Control Costs—The process of monitoring the
status of the project to update the project costs and
managing changes to the cost baseline.

94. Answer: A.

PMBOK® Guide, pages 198–200, Section 7.1.3.1

Cost Management Plan

The cost management plan is a component of the project management plan and describes how the project costs will be planned, structured, and controlled. The cost management processes and their associated tools and techniques are documented in the cost management plan.

For example, the cost management plan can establish the following:

- **Units of measure...**
- **Level of precision.** The degree to which activity cost estimates will be rounded up or down (e.g., US$100.49 to US$100, or US$995.59 to US$1,000), based on the scope of the activities and magnitude of the project.
- **Level of accuracy.** The acceptable range (e.g., 610%) used in determining realistic activity cost estimates is specified, and may include an amount for contingencies.
- **Organizational procedures links...**
- **Control thresholds.** Variance thresholds for monitoring cost performance may be specified to indicate an agreed-upon amount of variation to be allowed before some action needs to be taken. Thresholds are typically expressed as percentage deviations from the baseline plan.
- **Rules of performance measurement...**
- **Reporting formats...**
- **Process descriptions...**
- **Additional details...**

95. Answer: C.
PMBOK® Guide, pages 200–202, Section 7.2; and page 203, Section 7.2.1.5

Estimate Costs
Estimate Costs is the process of developing an approximation of the monetary resources needed to complete project activities. The key benefit of this process is that it determines the amount of cost required to complete project work...

Cost estimates are generally expressed in units of some currency (i.e., dollars, euros, yen, etc.), although in some instances other units of measure, such as staff hours or staff days, are used to facilitate comparisons by eliminating the effects of currency fluctuations...

Costs are estimated for all resources that will be charged to the project. This includes, but is not limited to, labor, materials, equipment, services, and facilities, as well as special categories such as an inflation allowance, cost of financing, or contingency costs. A cost estimate is a quantitative assessment of the likely costs for resources required to complete the activity. Cost estimates may be presented at the activity level or in summary form.

Risk Register
Described in Section 11.2.3.1. The risk register should be reviewed to consider risk response costs. Risks, which can be either threats or opportunities, typically have an impact on both activity and overall project costs. As a general rule, when the project experiences a negative risk event, the near-term cost of the project will usually increase, and there will sometimes be a delay in the project schedule. In a similar way, the project team should be sensitive to potential opportunities that can benefit the business either by directly reducing activity costs or by accelerating the schedule.

96. Answer: D.
PMBOK® Guide, page 202, Section 7.2

Estimate Costs
Costs are estimated for all resources that will be charged to the project. This includes, but is not limited to, labor, materials, equipment, services, and facilities, as well as special categories such as an inflation allowance, cost of financing, or contingency costs. A cost estimate is a quantitative assessment of the likely costs for resources required to complete the activity. Cost estimates may be presented at the activity level or in summary form.

97. Answer: C.
PMBOK® Guide, page 205, Section 7.2.2.3

Parametric Estimating
Parametric estimating uses a statistical relationship between relevant historical data and other variables (e.g., square footage in construction) to calculate a cost estimate for project work. This technique can produce higher levels of accuracy depending upon the sophistication and underlying data built into the model. Parametric cost estimates can be applied to a total project or to segments of a project, in conjunction with other estimating methods.

98. Answer: B.

PMBOK® Guide, page 204, Section 7.2.2.2

Analogous Estimating

Analogous cost estimating uses the values such as scope, cost, budget, and duration or measures of scale such as size, weight, and complexity from a previous, similar project as the basis for estimating the same parameter or measurement for a current project. When estimating costs, this technique relies on the actual cost of previous, similar projects as the basis for estimating the cost of the current project. It is a gross value estimating approach, sometimes adjusted for known differences in project complexity.

Analogous cost estimating is frequently used to estimate a value when there is a limited amount of detailed information about the project, for example, in the early phases of a project. Analogous cost estimating uses historical information and expert judgment.

Analogous cost estimating is generally less costly and less time consuming than other techniques, but it is also generally less accurate. Analogous cost estimates can be applied to a total project or to segments of a project, in conjunction with other estimating methods. Analogous estimating is most reliable when the previous projects are similar in fact and not just in appearance, and the project team members preparing the estimates have the needed expertise.

99. Answer: C.

PMBOK® Guide, page 208, Section 7.3; and pages 215–216, Section 7.4

Determine Budget

Determine Budget is the process of aggregating the estimated costs of individual activities or work packages to establish an authorized cost baseline. The key benefit of this process is that it determines the cost baseline against which project performance can be monitored and controlled.

Control Costs

Control Costs is the process of monitoring the status of the project to update the project costs and managing changes to the cost baseline. The key benefit of this process is that it provides the means to recognize variance from the plan in order to take corrective action and minimize risk.

… The key to effective cost control is the management of the approved cost baseline and the changes to that baseline.

Project cost control includes:
- Influencing the factors that create changes to the authorized cost baseline…

100. Answer: B.

PMBOK® Guide, pages 212–214, Section 7.3.3.1, Figure 7-8, and Figure 7-9

Cost Baseline

The cost baseline is the approved version of the time-phased project budget, excluding any management reserves, which can only be changed through formal change control procedures and is used as a basis for comparison to actual results. It is developed as a summation of the approved budgets for the different schedule activities.

Figure 7-8 illustrates the various components of the project budget and cost baseline. Activity cost estimates for the various project activities along with any contingency reserves (Section 7.2.2.6) for these activities are aggregated into their associated work package costs. The work package cost estimates, along with any contingency reserves estimated for the work packages, are aggregated into control accounts. The summation of the control accounts make up the cost baseline. Since the cost estimates that make up the cost baseline are directly tied to the schedule activities, this enables a time-phased view of the cost baseline, which is typically displayed in the form of an S-curve, as is illustrated in Figure 7-9.

Management reserves (Section 7.2.2.6) are added to the cost baseline to produce the project budget. As changes warranting the use of management reserves arise, the change control process is used to obtain approval to move the applicable management reserve funds into the cost baseline.

101. Answer: D.
PMBOK® Guide, page 216, Section 7.4

Determine Budget
Determine Budget is the process of aggregating the estimated costs of individual activities or work packages to establish an authorized cost baseline. The key benefit of this process is that it determines the cost baseline against which project performance can be monitored and controlled.

Control Costs
Project cost control includes:
- Influencing the factors that create changes to the authorized cost baseline;
- Ensuring that all change requests are acted on in a timely manner;
- Managing the actual changes when and as they occur;
- Ensuring that cost expenditures do not exceed the authorized funding by period, by WBS component, by activity, and in total for the project;
- Monitoring cost performance to isolate and understand variances from the approved cost baseline;
- Monitoring work performance against funds expended;
- Preventing unapproved changes from being included in the reported cost or resource usage;
- Informing appropriate stakeholders of all approved changes and associated cost; and
- Bringing expected cost overruns within acceptable limits.

102. Answer: B.
PMBOK® Guide, page 219, Section 7.4.2.1 and Figure 7-12

Earned Value Management
...
- **Schedule performance index.** The schedule performance index (SPI) is a measure of schedule efficiency expressed as the ratio of earned value to planned value. It measures how efficiently the project team is using its time. It is sometimes used in conjunction with the cost performance index (CPI) to forecast the final project completion estimates. An SPI value less than 1.0 indicates less work was completed than was planned. An SPI greater than 1.0 indicates that more work was completed than was planned. Since the SPI measures all project work, the performance on the critical path also needs to be analyzed to determine whether the project will finish ahead of or behind its planned finish date. The SPI is equal to the ratio of the EV to the PV. *Equation:* $SPI = EV/PV$
- **Cost performance index.** The cost performance index (CPI) is a measure of the cost efficiency of budgeted resources, expressed as a ratio of earned value to actual cost. It is considered the most critical EVM metric and measures the cost efficiency for the work completed. A CPI value of less than 1.0 indicates a cost overrun for work completed. A CPI value greater than 1.0 indicates a cost underrun of performance to date. The CPI is equal to the ratio of the EV to the AC. The indices are useful for determining project status and providing a basis for estimating project cost and schedule outcome. *Equation:* $CPI = EV/AC$

The three parameters of planned value, earned value, and actual cost can be monitored and reported on both a period-by-period basis (typically weekly or monthly) and on a cumulative basis. Figure 7-12 uses S-curves to display EV data for a project that is performing over budget and behind the schedule.

103. Answer: C.

PMBOK® Guide, page 220, Section 7.4.2.2

Forecasting

. . .

The project manager's manual EAC is quickly compared with a range of calculated EACs representing various risk scenarios. When calculating EAC values, the cumulative CPI and SPI values are typically used. While EVM data quickly provide many statistical EACs, only three of the more common methods are described as follows:

- **EAC forecast for ETC work performed at the budgeted rate.** This EAC method accepts the actual project performance to date (whether favorable or unfavorable) as represented by the actual costs, and predicts that all future ETC work will be accomplished at the budgeted rate. When actual performance is unfavorable, the assumption that future performance will improve should be accepted only when supported by project risk analysis. *Equation:* $EAC = AC + (BAC - EV)$

104. Answer: A.

PMBOK® Guide, page 220, Section 7.4.2.2

Forecasting

. . .

The project manager's manual EAC is quickly compared with a range of calculated EACs representing various risk scenarios. When calculating EAC values, the cumulative CPI and SPI values are typically used. While EVM data quickly provide many statistical EACs, only three of the more common methods are described as follows:

- **EAC forecast for ETC work performed at the present CPI.** This method assumes what the project has experienced to date can be expected to continue in the future. The ETC work is assumed to be performed at the same cumulative cost performance index (CPI) as that incurred by the project to date. *Equation:* $EAC = BAC/CPI$

105. Answer: D.

PMBOK® Guide, page 221, Section 7.4.2.2

Forecasting

…

The project manager's manual EAC is quickly compared with a range of calculated EACs representing various risk scenarios. When calculating EAC values, the cumulative CPI and SPI values are typically used. While EVM data quickly provide many statistical EACs, only three of the more common methods are described as follows:

…

- **EAC forecast for ETC work considering both SPI and CPI factors.** In this forecast, the ETC work will be performed at an efficiency rate that considers both the cost and schedule performance indices. This method is most useful when the project schedule is a factor impacting the ETC effort. Variations of this method weight the CPI and SPI at different values (e.g., 80/20, 50/50, or some other ratio) according to the project manager's judgment. *Equation:* $EAC = AC + [(BAC - EV)/(CPI \times SPI)]$

106. Answer: B.

PMBOK® Guide, page 220, Section 7.4.2.2; and page 224, Table 7-1

Forecasting

...

The project manager's manual EAC is quickly compared with a range of calculated EACs representing various risk scenarios. When calculating EAC values, the cumulative CPI and SPI values are typically used. While EVM data quickly provide many statistical EACs, only three of the more common methods are described as follows:

...

- **EAC forecast for ETC work performed at the present CPI.** This method assumes what the project has experienced to date can be expected to continue in the future. The ETC work is assumed to be performed at the same cumulative cost performance index (CPI) as that incurred by the project to date. *Equation:* $EAC = BAC/CPI$

Equation: $VAC = BAC - EAC$

107. Answer: A.

PMBOK® Guide, page 220, Section 7.4.2.2; and page 224, Table 7-1

Forecasting

…

The project manager's manual EAC is quickly compared with a range of calculated EACs representing various risk scenarios. When calculating EAC values, the cumulative CPI and SPI values are typically used. While EVM data quickly provide many statistical EACs, only three of the more common methods are described as follows:

- **EAC forecast for ETC work performed at the budgeted rate.** This EAC method accepts the actual project performance to date (whether favorable or unfavorable) as represented by the actual costs, and predicts that all future ETC work will be accomplished at the budgeted rate. When actual performance is unfavorable, the assumption that future performance will improve should be accepted only when supported by project risk analysis. *Equation:* $EAC = AC + (BAC - EV)$

Equation: $ETC = EAC - AC$

108. Answer: C.
PMBOK® Guide, page 221, Section 7.4.2.3; page 222, Figure 7-13; and page 224, Table 7-1

To-Complete Performance Index (TCPI)
The to-complete performance index (TCPI) is a measure of the cost performance that is required to be achieved with the remaining resources in order to meet a specified management goal, expressed as the ratio of the cost to finish the outstanding work to the remaining budget. TCPI is the calculated cost performance index that is achieved on the remaining work to meet a specified management goal, such as the BAC or the EAC. If it becomes obvious that the BAC is no longer viable, the project manager should consider the forecasted EAC. Once approved, the EAC may replace the BAC in the TCPI calculation. The equation for the TCPI based on the BAC: $(BAC - EV)/(BAC - AC)$.

The TCPI is conceptually displayed in Figure 7-13. The equation for the TCPI is shown in the lower left as the work remaining (defined as the BAC minus the EV) divided by the funds remaining (which can be either the BAC minus the AC, or the EAC minus the AC).

If the cumulative CPI falls below the baseline (as shown in Figure 7-13), all future work of the project will need to be performed immediately in the range of the TCPI (BAC) (as reflected in the top line of Figure 7-13) to stay within the authorized BAC. Whether this level of performance is achievable is a judgment call based on a number of considerations, including risk, schedule, and technical performance. This level of performance is displayed as the TCPI (EAC) line. The equation for the TCPI based on the EAC: $(BAC - EV)/(EAC - AC)$. The EVM formulas are provided in Table 7-1.

Equation: $TCPI = (BAC - EV)/(BAC - AC)$

109. Answer: A.

PMBOK® Guide, page 220, Section 7.4.2.2

Forecasting

As the project progresses, the project team may develop a forecast for the estimate at completion (EAC) that may differ from the budget at completion (BAC) based on the project performance. If it becomes obvious that the BAC is no longer viable, the project manager should consider the forecasted EAC. Forecasting the EAC involves making projections of conditions and events in the project's future based on current performance information and other knowledge available at the time of the forecast. Forecasts are generated, updated, and reissued based on work performance data (Section 4.3.3.2) that is provided as the project is executed. The work performance information covers the project's past performance and any information that could impact the project in the future.

EACs are typically based on the actual costs incurred for work completed, plus an estimate to complete (ETC) the remaining work. It is incumbent on the project team to predict what it may encounter to perform the ETC, based on its experience to date...

110. Answer: C.

PMBOK® Guide, pages 218–219, Section 7.4.2.1 and Figure 7-12

Earned Value Management

…

Variances from the approved baseline will also be monitored:

- **Schedule variance.** Schedule variance (SV) is a measure of schedule performance expressed as the difference between the earned value and the planned value. It is the amount by which the project is ahead or behind the planned delivery date, at a given point in time. It is a measure of schedule performance on a project. It is equal to the earned value (EV) minus the planned value (PV). The EVM schedule variance is a useful metric in that it can indicate when a project is falling behind or is ahead of its baseline schedule. The EVM schedule variance will ultimately equal zero when the project is completed because all of the planned values will have been earned. Schedule variance is best used in conjunction with critical path methodology (CPM) scheduling and risk management. *Equation:* $SV = EV - PV$

…

The SV and CV values can be converted to efficiency indicators to reflect the cost and schedule performance of any project for comparison against all other projects or within a portfolio of projects. The variances are useful for determining project status.

- **Schedule performance index.** The schedule performance index (SPI) is a measure of schedule efficiency expressed as the ratio of earned value to planned value. It measures how efficiently the project team is using its time. It is sometimes used in conjunction with the cost performance index (CPI) to forecast the final project completion estimates. An SPI value less than 1.0 indicates less work was completed than was planned. An SPI greater than 1.0 indicates that more work was completed than was planned. Since the SPI measures all project work, the performance on the critical path also needs to be analyzed to determine whether the project will finish ahead of or behind its planned finish date. The SPI is equal to the ratio of the EV to the PV. *Equation:* SPI = EV/PV

...

The three parameters of planned value, earned value, and actual cost can be monitored and reported on both a period-by-period basis (typically weekly or monthly) and on a cumulative basis. Figure 7-12 uses S-curves to display EV data for a project that is performing over budget and behind the schedule.

111. Answer: A.

PMBOK® Guide, pages 218–219, Section 7.4.2.1 and Figure 7-12

Earned Value Management

...

Variances from the approved baseline will also be monitored:

...

- **Cost variance.** Cost variance (CV) is the amount of budget deficit or surplus at a given point in time, expressed as the difference between earned value and the actual cost. It is a measure of cost performance on a project. It is equal to the earned value (EV) minus the actual cost (AC). The cost variance at the end of the project will be the difference between the budget at completion (BAC) and the actual amount spent. The CV is particularly critical because it indicates the relationship of physical performance to the costs spent. Negative CV is often difficult for the project to recover. *Equation:* $CV = EV - AC$

The SV and CV values can be converted to efficiency indicators to reflect the cost and schedule performance of any project for comparison against all other projects or within a portfolio of projects. The variances are useful for determining project status.

...

- **Cost performance index.** The cost performance index (CPI) is a measure of the cost efficiency of budgeted resources, expressed as a ratio of earned value to actual cost. It is considered the most critical EVM metric and measures the cost efficiency for the work completed. A CPI value of less than 1.0 indicates a cost overrun for work completed. A CPI value greater than 1.0 indicates a cost underrun of performance to date. The CPI is equal to the ratio of the EV to the AC. The indices are useful for determining project status and providing a basis for estimating project cost and schedule outcome. *Equation:* $CPI = EV/AC$

The three parameters of planned value, earned value, and actual cost can be monitored and reported on both a period-by-period basis (typically weekly or monthly) and on a cumulative basis. Figure 7-12 uses S-curves to display EV data for a project that is performing over budget and behind the schedule.

112. Answer: C.
PMBOK® Guide, page 217, Section 7.4.2.1

Earned Value Management
Earned value management (EVM) is a methodology that combines scope, schedule, and resource measurements to assess project performance and progress. It is a commonly used method of performance measurement for projects. It integrates the scope baseline with the cost baseline, along with the schedule baseline, to form the performance baseline, which helps the project management team assess and measure project performance and progress. It is a project management technique that requires the formation of an integrated baseline against which performance can be measured for the duration of the project. The principles of EVM can be applied to all projects in any industry.

113. Answer: D.

PMBOK® Guide, pages 218–219, Section 7.4.2.1 and Figure 7-12

Earned Value Management

...

Variances from the approved baseline will also be monitored:

- **Schedule variance.** Schedule variance (SV) is a measure of schedule performance expressed as the difference between the earned value and the planned value. It is the amount by which the project is ahead or behind the planned delivery date, at a given point in time. It is a measure of schedule performance on a project. It is equal to the earned value (EV) minus the planned value (PV). The EVM schedule variance is a useful metric in that it can indicate when a project is falling behind or is ahead of its baseline schedule. The EVM schedule variance will ultimately equal zero when the project is completed because all of the planned values will have been earned. Schedule variance is best used in conjunction with critical path methodology (CPM) scheduling and risk management. *Equation:* SV = EV − PV

- **Cost variance.** Cost variance (CV) is the amount of budget deficit or surplus at a given point in time, expressed as the difference between earned value and the actual cost. It is a measure of cost performance on a project. It is equal to the earned value (EV) minus the actual cost (AC). The cost variance at the end of the project will be the difference between the budget at completion (BAC) and the actual amount spent. The CV is particularly critical because it indicates the relationship of physical performance to the costs spent. Negative CV is often difficult for the project to recover. *Equation:* CV = EV − AC

The SV and CV values can be converted to efficiency indicators to reflect the cost and schedule performance of any project for comparison against all other projects or within a portfolio of projects. The variances are useful for determining project status.

- **Schedule performance index.** The schedule performance index (SPI) is a measure of schedule efficiency expressed as the ratio of earned value to planned value. It measures how efficiently the project team is using its time. It is sometimes used in conjunction with the cost performance index (CPI) to forecast the final project completion estimates. An SPI value less than 1.0 indicates less work was completed than was planned. An SPI greater than 1.0 indicates that more work was completed than was planned. Since the SPI measures all project work, the performance on the critical path also needs to be analyzed to determine whether the project will finish ahead of or behind its planned finish date. The SPI is equal to the ratio of the EV to the PV. *Equation:* $SPI = EV/PV$
- **Cost performance index.** The cost performance index (CPI) is a measure of the cost efficiency of budgeted resources, expressed as a ratio of earned value to actual cost. It is considered the most critical EVM metric and measures the cost efficiency for the work completed. A CPI value of less than 1.0 indicates a cost overrun for work completed. A CPI value greater than 1.0 indicates a cost underrun of performance to date. The CPI is equal to the ratio of the EV to the AC. The indices are useful for determining project status and providing a basis for estimating project cost and schedule outcome. *Equation*: $CPI = EV/AC$

The three parameters of planned value, earned value, and actual cost can be monitored and reported on both a period-by-period basis (typically weekly or monthly) and on a cumulative basis. Figure 7-12 uses S-curves to display EV data for a project that is performing over budget and behind the schedule.

114. Answer: B.

PMBOK® Guide, page 218, Section 7.4.2.1

Earned Value Management

...

Variances from the approved baseline will also be monitored:

...

• **Cost variance.** Cost variance (CV) is the amount of budget deficit or surplus at a given point in time, expressed as the difference between earned value and the actual cost. It is a measure of cost performance on a project. It is equal to the earned value (EV) minus the actual cost (AC). The cost variance at the end of the project will be the difference between the budget at completion (BAC) and the actual amount spent. The CV is particularly critical because it indicates the relationship of physical performance to the costs spent. Negative CV is often difficult for the project to recover. *Equation:* $CV = EV - AC$

115. Answer: B.
PMBOK® Guide, pages 218–219, Section 7.4.2.1

Earned Value Management
… EVM develops and monitors three key dimensions for each work package and control account:

…

- **Earned value.** Earned value (EV) is a measure of work performed expressed in terms of the budget authorized for that work. It is the budget associated with the authorized work that has been completed. The EV being measured needs to be related to the PMB, and the EV measured cannot be greater than the authorized PV budget for a component. The EV is often used to calculate the percent complete of a project. Progress measurement criteria should be established for each WBS component to measure work in progress. Project managers monitor EV, both incrementally to determine current status and cumulatively to determine the long-term performance trends.

116. Answer: B.
PMBOK® Guide, page 219, Section 7.4.2.1 and Figure 7-12

Earned Value Management

...
- **Schedule performance index.** The schedule performance index (SPI) is a measure of schedule efficiency expressed as the ratio of earned value to planned value. It measures how efficiently the project team is using its time. It is sometimes used in conjunction with the cost performance index (CPI) to forecast the final project completion estimates. An SPI value less than 1.0 indicates less work was completed than was planned. An SPI greater than 1.0 indicates that more work was completed than was planned. Since the SPI measures all project work, the performance on the critical path also needs to be analyzed to determine whether the project will finish ahead of or behind its planned finish date. The SPI is equal to the ratio of the EV to the PV. *Equation:* SPI = EV/PV
- **Cost performance index.** The cost performance index (CPI) is a measure of the cost efficiency of budgeted resources, expressed as a ratio of earned value to actual cost. It is considered the most critical EVM metric and measures the cost efficiency for the work completed. A CPI value of less than 1.0 indicates a cost overrun for work completed. A CPI value greater than 1.0 indicates a cost underrun of performance to date. The CPI is equal to the ratio of the EV to the AC. The indices are useful for determining project status and providing a basis for estimating project cost and schedule outcome. *Equation:* CPI = EV/AC

The three parameters of planned value, earned value, and actual cost can be monitored and reported on both a period-by-period basis (typically weekly or monthly) and on a cumulative basis. Figure 7-12 uses S-curves to display EV data for a project that is performing over budget and behind the schedule.

117. Answer: D.

PMBOK® Guide, pages 218–219, Section 7.4.2.1 and Figure 7-12

Earned Value Management

…

Variances from the approved baseline will also be monitored:

…

- **Cost variance.** Cost variance (CV) is the amount of budget deficit or surplus at a given point in time, expressed as the difference between earned value and the actual cost. It is a measure of cost performance on a project. It is equal to the earned value (EV) minus the actual cost (AC). The cost variance at the end of the project will be the difference between the budget at completion (BAC) and the actual amount spent. The CV is particularly critical because it indicates the relationship of physical performance to the costs spent. Negative CV is often difficult for the project to recover. *Equation:* $CV = EV - AC$

The SV and CV values can be converted to efficiency indicators to reflect the cost and schedule performance of any project for comparison against all other projects or within a portfolio of projects. The variances are useful for determining project status.

…

- **Cost performance index.** The cost performance index (CPI) is a measure of the cost efficiency of budgeted resources, expressed as a ratio of earned value to actual cost. It is considered the most critical EVM metric and measures the cost efficiency for the work completed. A CPI value of less than 1.0 indicates a cost overrun for work completed. A CPI value greater than 1.0 indicates a cost underrun of performance to date. The CPI is equal to the ratio of the EV to the AC. The indices are useful for determining project status and providing a basis for estimating project cost and schedule outcome. *Equation:* $CPI = EV/AC$

The three parameters of planned value, earned value, and actual cost can be monitored and reported on both a period-by-period basis (typically weekly or monthly) and on a cumulative basis. Figure 7-12 uses S-curves to display EV data for a project that is performing over budget and behind the schedule.

118. Answer: D.

PMBOK® Guide, page 219, Section 7.4.2.1 and Figure 7-12

Earned Value Management

…

The SV and CV values can be converted to efficiency indicators to reflect the cost and schedule performance of any project for comparison against all other projects or within a portfolio of projects. The variances are useful for determining project status.

- **Schedule performance index.** The schedule performance index (SPI) is a measure of schedule efficiency expressed as the ratio of earned value to planned value. It measures how efficiently the project team is using its time. It is sometimes used in conjunction with the cost performance index (CPI) to forecast the final project completion estimates. An SPI value less than 1.0 indicates less work was completed than was planned. An SPI greater than 1.0 indicates that more work was completed than was planned. Since the SPI measures all project work, the performance on the critical path also needs to be analyzed to determine whether the project will finish ahead of or behind its planned finish date. The SPI is equal to the ratio of the EV to the PV. *Equation:* SPI $=$ EV/PV

…

The three parameters of planned value, earned value, and actual cost can be monitored and reported on both a period-by-period basis (typically weekly or monthly) and on a cumulative basis. Figure 7-12 uses S-curves to display EV data for a project that is performing over budget and behind the schedule.

Project Quality Management

(Chapter 8 of the *PMBOK® Guide*)

119. Answer: A.

PMBOK® Guide, page 227, Introduction

Project Quality Management

Project Quality Management includes the processes and activities of the performing organization that determine quality policies, objectives, and responsibilities so that the project will satisfy the needs for which it was undertaken. Project Quality Management uses policies and procedures to implement, within the project's context, the organization's quality management system and, as appropriate, it supports continuous process improvement activities as undertaken on behalf of the performing organization. Project Quality Management works to ensure that the project requirements, including product requirements, are met and validated.

120. Answer: A.

PMBOK® Guide, page 228, Introduction

Project Quality Management

Quality and *grade* are not the same concepts. Quality as a delivered performance or result is "the degree to which a set of inherent characteristics fulfill requirements" (ISO 9000)[10]. Grade as a design intent is a category assigned to deliverables having the same functional use but different technical characteristics. The project manager and the project management team are responsible for managing the tradeoffs associated with delivering the required levels of both quality and grade. While a quality level that fails to meet quality requirements is always a problem, a low grade of quality may not be a problem. For example:

- It may not be a problem if a suitable low-grade software product (one with a limited number of features) is of high quality (no obvious defects, readable manual). In this example, the product would be appropriate for its general purpose of use.
- It may be a problem if a high-grade software product (one with numerous features) is of low quality (many defects, poorly organized user documentation). In essence, its high-grade feature set would prove ineffective and/or inefficient due to its low quality.

121. Answer: A.
PMBOK® Guide, page 229, Introduction

Project Quality Management
...

In the context of achieving ISO compatibility, modern quality management approaches seek to minimize variation and to deliver results that meet defined requirements. These approaches recognize the importance of:
- **Customer satisfaction.** Understanding, evaluating, defining, and managing requirements so that customer expectations are met. This requires a combination of conformance to requirements (to ensure the project produces what it was created to produce) and fitness for use (the product or service needs to satisfy the real needs).

122. Answer: C.
PMBOK® Guide, page 229, Introduction

Project Quality Management
...

In the context of achieving ISO compatibility, modern quality management approaches seek to minimize variation and to deliver results that meet defined requirements. These approaches recognize the importance of:
- **Prevention over inspection.** Quality should be planned, designed, and built into—not inspected into the project's management or the project's deliverables. The cost of preventing mistakes is generally much less than the cost of correcting mistakes when they are found by inspection or during usage.

123. Answer: D.
PMBOK® Guide, page 235, Section 8.1.2.1

Cost-Benefit Analysis
The primary benefits of meeting quality requirements include less rework, higher productivity, lower costs, increased stakeholder satisfaction, and increased profitability. A cost-benefit analysis for each quality activity compares the cost of the quality step to the expected benefit.

124. Answer: D.
PMBOK® Guide, pages 250–251, Section 8.3.1; and page 249, Figure 8-11

Control Quality: Inputs
.1 Project Management Plan
.2 Quality Metrics
.3 Quality Checklists
.4 Work Performance Data
.5 Approved Change Requests
.6 Deliverables
.7 Project Documents
.8 Organizational Process Assets

125. Answer: B.
PMBOK® Guide, pages 239–240, Section 8.1.2.5

Design of Experiments
Design of experiments (DOE) is a statistical method
for identifying which factors may influence specific
variables of a product or process under development
or in production. DOE may be used during the Plan
Quality Management process to determine the number
and type of tests and their impact on cost of quality.

DOE also plays a role in optimizing products or
processes. DOE is used to reduce the sensitivity of
product performance to sources of variations caused
by environmental or manufacturing differences. One
important aspect of this technique is that it provides a
statistical framework for systematically changing all of
the important factors, rather than changing the factors
one at a time. Analysis of the experimental data should
provide the optimal conditions for the product or
process, highlight the factors that influence the results,
and reveal the presence of interactions and synergy
among the factors. For example, automotive designers
use this technique to determine which combination of
suspension and tires will produce the most desirable
ride characteristics at a reasonable cost.

126. Answer: A.
PMBOK® Guide, page 241, Section 8.1.3.1

Quality Management Plan
The quality management plan is a component of the project management plan that describes how the organization's quality policies will be implemented. It describes how the project management team plans to meet the quality requirements set for the project.

The quality management plan may be formal or informal, detailed, or broadly framed. The style and detail of the quality management plan are determined by the requirements of the project. The quality management plan should be reviewed early in the project to ensure that decisions are based on accurate information. The benefits of this review can include a sharper focus on the project's value proposition and reductions in costs and in the frequency of schedule overruns that were caused by rework.

127. Answer: C.
PMBOK® Guide, page 242, Section 8.2

Perform Quality Assurance
Perform quality assurance is the process of auditing the quality requirements and the results from quality control measurements to ensure that appropriate quality standards and operational definitions are used. The key benefit of this process is that it facilitates the improvement of quality processes.

128. Answer: D.

PMBOK® Guide, page 237, Section 8.1.2.3; and page 239, Figure 8-7

- *Pareto diagrams,* exist as a special form of vertical bar chart and are used to identify the vital few sources that are responsible for causing most of a problem's effects. The categories shown on the horizontal axis exist as a valid probability distribution that accounts for 100% of the possible observations. The relative frequencies of each specified cause listed on the horizontal axis decrease in magnitude until the default source named "*other*" accounts for any nonspecified causes. Typically, the Pareto diagram will be organized into categories that measure either frequencies or consequences.

129. Answer: D.

PMBOK® Guide, page 235, Section 8.1.2.2 and Figure 8-5

Cost of Quality (COQ)

Cost of quality includes all costs incurred over the life of the product by investment in preventing nonconformance to requirements, appraising the product or service for conformance to requirements, and failing to meet requirements (rework). Failure costs are often categorized into internal (found by the project) and external (found by the customer). Failure costs are also called cost of poor quality. Figure 8-5 provides some examples to consider in each area.

130. Answer: A.

PMBOK® Guide, page 229, Introduction; and page 235, Figure 8-5

- **Cost of quality (COQ).** Cost of quality refers to the total cost of the conformance work and the nonconformance work that should be done as a compensatory effort because, on the first attempt to perform that work, the potential exists that some portion of the required work effort may be done or has been done incorrectly. The costs for quality work may be incurred throughout the deliverable's life cycle. For example, decisions made by the project team can impact the operational costs associated with using a completed deliverable. Post-project quality costs may be incurred because of product returns, warranty claims, and recall campaigns. Therefore, because of the temporary nature of projects and the potential benefits that may be derived from reducing the post-project cost of quality, sponsoring organizations may choose to invest in product quality improvement. These investments generally are made in the areas of conformance work that act to prevent defects or act to mitigate the costs of defects by inspecting out nonconforming units. Refer to Figure 8-2 and Section 8.1.2.2. Moreover, the issues related to post-project COQ should be the concern of program management and portfolio management such that project, program, and portfolio management offices should apply appropriate reviews, templates, and funding allocations for this purpose.

131. Answer: D.

PMBOK® Guide, pages 236–238, Section 8.1.2.3; and page 239, Figure 8-7

Seven Basic Quality Tools

The seven basic quality tools, also known in the industry as 7QC Tools, are used within the context of the PDCA Cycle to solve quality-related problems. As conceptually illustrated in Figure 8-7, the seven basic quality tools are:

- *Cause-and-effect diagrams...*
- *Flowcharts...*
- *Checksheets...*
- *Pareto diagrams...*
- *Histograms...*
- *Control charts...*
- *Scatter diagram...*

132. Answer: C.

PMBOK® Guide, page 238, Section 8.1.2.3; page 239, Figures 8-7; and Glossary

- *Control charts,* are used to determine whether or not a process is stable or has predictable performance. Upper and lower specification limits are based on requirements of the agreement. They reflect the maximum and minimum values allowed. There may be penalties associated with exceeding the specification limits. Upper and lower control limits are different from specification limits. The control limits are determined using standard statistical calculations and principles to ultimately establish the natural capability for a stable process. The project manager and appropriate stakeholders may use the statistically calculated control limits to identify the points at which corrective action will be taken to prevent unnatural performance. The corrective action typically seeks to maintain the natural stability of a stable and capable process. For repetitive processes, the control limits are generally set at ±3 s around a process mean that has been set at 0 s. A process is considered out of control when: (1) a data point exceeds a control limit; (2) seven consecutive plot points are above the mean; or (3) seven consecutive plot points are below the mean.

Control charts can be used to monitor various types of output variables. Although used most frequently to track repetitive activities required for producing manufactured lots, control charts may also be used to monitor cost and schedule variances, volume, and frequency of scope changes, or other management results to help determine if the project management processes are in control.

Control Chart. A graphic display of process data over time and against established control limits, which has a centerline that assists in detecting a trend of plotted values toward either control limit.

133. Answer: A.

PMBOK® Guide, page 238, Section 8.1.2.3; and page 239, Figures 8-7

- *Control charts,* are used to determine whether or not a process is stable or has predictable performance. Upper and lower specification limits are based on requirements of the agreement. They reflect the maximum and minimum values allowed. There may be penalties associated with exceeding the specification limits. Upper and lower control limits are different from specification limits. The control limits are determined using standard statistical calculations and principles to ultimately establish the natural capability for a stable process. The project manager and appropriate stakeholders may use the statistically calculated control limits to identify the points at which corrective action will be taken to prevent unnatural performance. The corrective action typically seeks to maintain the natural stability of a stable and capable process. For repetitive processes, the control limits are generally set at ± 3 s around a process mean that has been set at 0 s. A process is considered out of control when: (1) a data point exceeds a control limit; (2) seven consecutive plot points are above the mean; or (3) seven consecutive plot points are below the mean.

134. Answer: B.

PMBOK® Guide, page 242, Section 8.2

Perform Quality Assurance

Perform quality assurance is the process of auditing the quality requirements and the results from quality control measurements to ensure that appropriate quality standards and operational definitions are used. The key benefit of this process is that it facilitates the improvement of quality processes.

135. Answer: B.
PMBOK® Guide, page 235, Section 8.1.2.1

Cost-Benefit Analysis
The primary benefits of meeting quality requirements include less rework, higher productivity, lower costs, increased stakeholder satisfaction, and increased profitability. A cost-benefit analysis for each quality activity compares the cost of the quality step to the expected benefit.

136. Answer: D.
PMBOK® Guide, page 239, Section 8.1.2.4

Benchmarking
Benchmarking involves comparing actual or planned project practices to those of comparable projects to identify best practices, generate ideas for improvement, and provide a basis for measuring performance.

Benchmarked projects may exist within the performing organization or outside of it, or can be within the same application area. Benchmarking allows for analogies from projects in a different application area to be made.

137. Answer D.

PMBOK® Guide, page 229, Introduction; and page 231, Figure 8-2

- **Continuous improvement.** The PDCA (plan-do-check-act) cycle is the basis for quality improvement as defined by Shewhart and modified by Deming. In addition, quality improvement initiatives such as Total Quality Management (TQM), Six Sigma, and Lean Six Sigma could improve the quality of the project's management as well as the quality of the project's product. Commonly used process improvement models include Malcolm Baldrige, Organizational Project Management Maturity Model (OPM3®), and Capability Maturity Model Integrated (CMMI®).

138. Answer: A.

PMBOK® Guide, page 229, Introduction; and page 231, Figure 8-2

- **Continuous improvement.** The PDCA (plan-do-check-act) cycle is the basis for quality improvement as defined by Shewhart and modified by Deming. In addition, quality improvement initiatives such as Total Quality Management (TQM), Six Sigma, and Lean Six Sigma could improve the quality of the project's management as well as the quality of the project's product. Commonly used process improvement models include Malcolm Baldrige, Organizational Project Management Maturity Model (OPM3®), and Capability Maturity Model Integrated (CMMI®).

139. Answer: A.

PMBOK® Guide, pages 245–246, Section 8.2.2.1 and Figure 8-10

- **Affinity diagrams.** The affinity diagram is similar to mind-mapping techniques in that they are used to generate ideas that can be linked to form organized patterns of thought about a problem. In project management, the creation of the WBS may be enhanced by using the affinity diagram to give structure to the decomposition of scope.

...

- **Prioritization matrices.** Identify the key issues and the suitable alternatives to be prioritized as a set of decisions for implementation. Criteria are prioritized and weighted before being applied to all available alternatives to obtain a mathematical score that ranks the options.

140. Answer: B.

PMBOK® Guide, page 228, Introduction

The project management team should determine the appropriate levels of accuracy and precision for use in the quality management plan. Precision is a measure of exactness. For example, the magnitude for each increment on the measurement's number line is the interval that determines the measurement's precision—the greater the number of increments, the greater the precision. Accuracy is an assessment of correctness. For example, if the measured value of an item is very close to the true value of the characteristic being measured, the measurement is more accurate. An illustration of this concept is the comparison of archery targets. Arrows clustered tightly in one area of the target, even if they are not clustered in the bull's-eye, are considered to have high precision. Targets where the arrows are more spread out but equidistant from the bull's-eye are considered to have the same degree of accuracy. Targets where the arrows are both tightly grouped and within the bull's-eye are considered to be both accurate and precise. Precise measurements are not necessarily accurate measurements, and accurate measurements are not necessarily precise measurements.

Project Human Resource Management

(Chapter 9 of the *PMBOK® Guide*)

141. Answer: D.

PMBOK® Guide, page 255, Introduction; and page 257, Figure 9-1

Project Human Resource Management

Figure 9-1 provides an overview of the Project Human Resource Management processes, which are as follows:

9.1 Plan Human Resource Management—The process of identifying and documenting project roles, responsibilities, required skills, reporting relationships, and creating a staffing management plan.

9.2 Acquire Project Team—The process of confirming human resource availability and obtaining the team necessary to complete project activities.

9.3 Develop Project Team—The process of improving competencies, team member interaction, and overall team environment to enhance project performance.

9.4 Manage Project Team—The process of tracking team member performance, providing feedback, resolving issues, and managing changes to optimize project performance.

142. Answer: C.

PMBOK® Guide, page 262, Section 9.1.2.1 and Figure 9-5

Matrix-based charts. A responsibility assignment matrix (RAM) is a grid that shows the project resources assigned to each work package. It is used to illustrate the connections between work packages or activities and project team members. On larger projects, RAMs can be developed at various levels. For example, a high-level RAM can define what a project team group or unit is responsible for within each component of the WBS, while lower-level RAMs are used within the group to designate roles, responsibilities, and levels of authority for specific activities. The matrix format shows all activities associated with one person and all people associated with one activity. This also ensures that there is only one person accountable for any one task to avoid confusion of responsibility. One example of a RAM is a RACI (responsible, accountable, consult, and inform) chart, shown in Figure 9-5. The sample chart shows the work to be done in the left column as activities. The assigned resources can be shown as individuals or groups. The project manager can select other options such as "lead" and "resource" designations or others, as appropriate for the project. A RACI chart is a useful tool to use when the team consists of internal and external resources in order to ensure clear divisions of roles and expectations.

143. Answer: D.

PMBOK® Guide, pages 264–265, Section 9.1.3

Plan Human Resource Management: Outputs
.1 Human Resource Management Plan

The human resource management plan, a part of the project management plan, provides guidance on how project human resources should be defined, staffed, managed, and eventually released. The human resource management plan and any subsequent revisions are also inputs into the Develop Project Management Plan process.

The human resource management plan includes, but is not limited to, the following:

- **Roles and responsibilities...**
- **Project organization charts...**
- **Staffing management plan...**

144. Answer: C.

PMBOK® Guide, page 265, Section 9.1.3.1

Staffing management plan. The staffing management plan is a component of the human resource management plan that describes when and how project team members will be acquired and how long they will be needed. It describes how human resource requirements will be met...

- *Staff acquisition.* A number of questions arise when planning the acquisition of project team members. For example, whether the human resources come from within the organization or from external, contracted sources; whether the team members need to work in a central location or may work from distant locations; costs associated with each level of expertise needed for the project; and level of assistance that the organization's human resource department and functional managers are able to provide to the project management team.

145. Answer: A.

PMBOK® Guide, page 265, Section 9.1.3.1; and page 266 Figure 9-6

> **Staffing management plan.** The staffing management plan is a component of the human resource management plan that describes when and how project team members will be acquired and how long they will be needed. It describes how human resource requirements will be met...
>
> - *Resource calendars.* Calendars that identify the working days and shifts on which each specific resource is available. The staffing management plan describes necessary time frames for project team members, either individually or collectively, as well as when acquisition activities such as recruiting should start. One tool for charting human resources is a resource histogram, used by the project management team as a means of providing a visual representation or resources allocation to all interested parties. This chart illustrates the number of hours a person, department, or entire project team that will be needed each week or month over the course of the project. The chart can include a horizontal line that represents the maximum number of hours available from a particular resource. Bars that extend beyond the maximum available hours identify the need for a resource optimization strategy (Section 6.6.2.4), such as adding more resources or modifying the schedule. An example of a resource histogram is illustrated in Figure 9-6.

146. Answer: B.

PMBOK® Guide, page 267, Section 9.2; and page 269, Section 9.2.1.2

Acquire Project Team

Acquire project team is the process of confirming human resource availability and obtaining the team necessary to complete project activities. The key benefit of this process consists of outlining and guiding the team selection and responsibility assignment to obtain a successful team...

Enterprise Environmental Factors

Described in Section 2.1.5. The enterprise environmental factors that influence the Acquire Project Team process include, but are not limited to:

- Existing information on human resources including availability, competency levels, prior experience, interest in working on the project and their cost rate;
- Personnel administration policies such as those that affect outsourcing;
- Organizational structure as described in Section 2.3.1; and
- Colocation or multiple locations.

147. Answer: C.

PMBOK® Guide, page 266, Section 9.1.3.1

- *Staff release plan.* Determining the method and timing of releasing team members benefits both the project and team members. When team members are released from a project, the costs associated with those resources are no longer charged to the project, thus reducing project costs. Morale is improved when smooth transitions to upcoming projects are already planned. A staff release plan also helps mitigate human resource risks that may occur during or at the end of a project.

148. Answer: D.
PMBOK® Guide, page 266, Section 9.1.3.1; and page 277, Section 9.3.2.6

> *Recognition and rewards.* Clear criteria for rewards and a planned system for their use help promote and reinforce desired behaviors. To be effective, recognition and rewards should be based on activities and performance under a person's control. For example, a team member who is to be rewarded for meeting cost objectives should have an appropriate level of control over decisions that affect expenses. Creating a plan with established times for distribution of rewards ensures that recognition takes place and is not forgotten...

> **Recognition and rewards**
> ... It is important to recognize that a particular reward given to any individual will be effective only if it satisfies a need which is valued by that individual... Cultural differences should be considered when determining recognition and rewards.

> People are motivated if they feel they are valued in the organization and this value is demonstrated by the rewards given to them. Generally, money is viewed as a tangible aspect of any reward system, but intangible rewards could be equally or even more effective. Most project team members are motivated by an opportunity to grow, accomplish, and apply their professional skills to meet new challenges. A good strategy for project managers is to give the team recognition throughout the life cycle of the project rather than waiting until the project is completed.

149. Answer: C.

PMBOK® Guide, page 267, Figure 9-7; and pages 270–271, Section 9.2.2

Acquire Project Team: Tools and Techniques
.1 Pre-assignment
.2 Negotiation
.3 Acquisition
.4 Virtual teams

150. Answer: B.

PMBOK® Guide, pages 275–277, Sections 9.3.2 and 9.3.2.5

Develop Project Team: Tools and Techniques
...

Colocation
Colocation, also referred to as "tight matrix," involves placing many or all of the most active project team members in the same physical location to enhance their ability to perform as a team. Colocation can be temporary, such as at strategically important times during the project, or for the entire project. Colocation strategies can include a team meeting room (sometimes called "war room"), places to post schedules, and other conveniences that enhance communication and a sense of community. While colocation is considered a good strategy, the use of virtual teams can bring benefits such as the use of more skilled resources, reduced costs, less travel, and relocation expenses and the proximity of team members to suppliers, customers, or other key stakeholders.

151. Answer: C.
PMBOK® Guide, pages 282–283, Section 9.4.2.3

Conflict Management

Conflict is inevitable in a project environment. Sources of conflict include scarce resources, scheduling priorities, and personal work styles. Team ground rules, group norms, and solid project management practices, like communication planning and role definition, reduce the amount of conflict.

Successful conflict management results in greater productivity and positive working relationships. When managed properly, differences of opinion can lead to increased creativity and better decision making. If the differences become a negative factor, project team members are initially responsible for their resolution. If conflict escalates, the project manager should help facilitate a satisfactory resolution. Conflict should be addressed early and usually in private, using a direct, collaborative approach. If disruptive conflict continues, formal procedures may be used, including disciplinary actions.

152. Answer: B.

PMBOK® Guide, page 276, Section 9.3.2.3; and Appendix X3, Section X3.2

Team-Building Activities

Team-building activities can vary from a 5-minute agenda item in a status review meeting to an off-site, professionally facilitated experience designed to improve interpersonal relationships. The objective of team-building activities is to help individual team members work together effectively. Team-building strategies are particularly valuable when team members operate from remote locations without the benefit of face-to-face contact. Informal communication and activities can help in building trust and establishing good working relationships.

As an ongoing process, team building is crucial to project success. While team building is essential during the initial stages of a project, it is a never-ending process. Changes in a project environment are inevitable, and to manage them effectively, a continued or a renewed team-building effort should be applied. The project manager should continually monitor team functionality and performance to determine if any actions are needed to prevent or correct various team problems.

Team Building

...

While team building is essential during the front end of a project, it is an ongoing process. Changes in a project environment are inevitable. To manage these changes effectively, a continued or renewed team-building effort is required. Outcomes of team building include mutual trust, high quality of information exchange, better decision making, and effective project management.

153. Answer: C.

PMBOK® Guide, page 275, Section 9.3.2.2

Training

Training includes all activities designed to enhance the competencies of the project team members. Training can be formal or informal. Examples of training methods include classroom, online, computer-based, on-the-job training from another project team member, mentoring, and coaching. If project team members lack the necessary management or technical skills, such skills can be developed as part of the project work. Scheduled training takes place as stated in the human resource management plan. Unplanned training takes place as a result of observation, conversation, and project performance appraisals conducted during the controlling process of managing the project team. Training costs could be included in the project budget, or supported by performing organization if the added skills may be useful for future projects. It could be performed by in-house or external trainers.

154. Answer: C.
PMBOK® Guide, page 278, Section 9.3.3.1

Team Performance Assessments

As project team development efforts such as training, team building, and colocation are implemented, the project management team makes formal or informal assessments of the project team's effectiveness. Effective team development strategies and activities are expected to increase the team's performance, which increases the likelihood of meeting project objectives...

The evaluation of a team's effectiveness may include indicators such as:
- Improvements in skills that allow individuals to perform assignments more effectively,
- Improvements in competencies that help the team perform better as a team,
- Reduced staff turnover rate, and
- Increased team cohesiveness where team members share information and experiences openly and help each other to improve the overall project performance.

155. Answer: B.

PMBOK® Guide, page 270, Section 9.2.2.2; and Appendix X3, Section X3.8

Negotiation

Staff assignments are negotiated on many projects. For example, the project management team may need to negotiate with:

- Functional managers, to ensure that the project receives appropriately competent staff in the required time frame and that the project team members will be able, willing, and authorized to work on the project until their responsibilities are completed;
- Other project management teams within the performing organization, to appropriately assign scarce or specialized human resources; and
- External organizations, vendors, suppliers, contractors, etc., for appropriate, scarce, specialized, qualified, certified, or other such specified human resources. Special consideration should be given to external negotiating policies, practices, processes, guidelines, legal, and other such criteria.

The project management team's ability to influence others plays an important role in negotiating staff assignments, as do the politics of the organizations involved...

Negotiation

Negotiation is a strategy of conferring with parties of shared or opposed interests with a view toward compromise or reaching an agreement. Negotiation is an integral part of project management and done well, increases the probability of project success.

156. Answer: C.

PMBOK® Guide, page 283, Section 9.4.2.3

Conflict Management

...

There are five general techniques for resolving conflict. As each one has its place and use, these are not given in any particular order:

- **Withdraw/Avoid.** Retreating from an actual or potential conflict situation; postponing the issue to be better prepared or to be resolved by others.
- **Smooth/Accommodate.** Emphasizing areas of agreement rather than areas of difference; conceding one's position to the needs of others to maintain harmony and relationships.
- **Compromise/Reconcile.** Searching for solutions that bring some degree of satisfaction to all parties in order to temporarily or partially resolve the conflict.
- **Force/Direct.** Pushing one's viewpoint at the expense of others; offering only win-lose solutions, usually enforced through a power position to resolve an emergency.
- **Collaborate/Problem Solve.** Incorporating multiple viewpoints and insights from differing perspectives; requires a cooperative attitude and open dialogue that typically leads to consensus and commitment.

157. Answer: A.
PMBOK® Guide, page 256, Introduction

Managing and leading the project team includes, but is not limited to:
- **Influencing the project team.** The project manager needs to be aware of and influence, when possible, human resource factors that may impact the project. These factors includes team environment, geographical locations of team members, communications among stakeholders, internal and external politics, cultural issues, organizational uniqueness, and others factors that may alter project performance.
- **Professional and ethical behavior.** The project management team should be aware of, subscribe to, and ensure that all team members follow professional and ethical behavior.

158. Answer: D.
PMBOK® Guide, page 263, Section 9.1.2.3

Organizational Theory
Organizational theory provides information regarding the way in which people, teams, and organizational units behave. Effective use of common themes identified in organizational theory can shorten the amount of time, cost, and effort needed to create the Plan Human Resource Management process outputs and improve planning efficiency. It is important to recognize that different organizational structures have different individual response, individual performance, and personal relationship characteristics. Also, applicable organizational theories may recommend exercising a flexible leadership style that adapts to the changes in a team's maturity level throughout the project life cycle.

159. Answer: B.
PMBOK® Guide, page 276, Section 9.3.2.3

Team-Building Activities
...
One of the models used to describe team development is the Tuckman ladder (Tuckman, 1965; Tuckman & Jensen, 1977), which includes five stages of development that teams may go through. Although it's common for these stages to occur in order, it's not uncommon for a team to get stuck in a particular stage or slip to an earlier stage. Projects with team members who worked together in the past may skip a stage.

- **Forming.** This phase is where the team meets and learns about the project and their formal roles and responsibilities. Team members tend to be independent and not as open in this phase.
- **Storming.** During this phase, the team begins to address the project work, technical decisions, and the project management approach. If team members are not collaborative and open to differing ideas and perspectives, the environment can become counterproductive.
- **Norming.** In the norming phase, team members begin to work together and adjust their work habits and behaviors to support the team. The team learns to trust each other.
- **Performing.** Teams that reach the performing stage function as a well-organized unit. They are interdependent and work through issues smoothly and effectively.
- **Adjourning.** In the adjourning phase, the team completes the work and moves on from the project. This typically occurs when staff is released from the project as deliverables are completed or as part of carrying out the Close Project or Phase process (Section 4.6).

The duration of a particular stage depends upon team dynamics, team size, and team leadership. Project managers should have a good understanding of team dynamics in order to move their team members through all stages in an effective manner.

160. Answer: C.

PMBOK® Guide, pages 283–284, Section 9.4.2.4; and Appendix X3

Interpersonal Skills

Project managers use a combination of technical, personal, and conceptual skills to analyze situations and interact appropriately with team members. Using appropriate interpersonal skills allows project managers to capitalize on the strengths of all team members.

Examples of interpersonal skills that a project manager uses most often include:
- **Leadership...**
- **Influencing...**
- **Effective decision making...**

Interpersonal Skills

Project managers accomplish work through the project team and other stakeholders. Effective project managers acquire a balance of technical, interpersonal, and conceptual skills that help them analyze situations and interact appropriately. This appendix describes important interpersonal skills, such as:
- Leadership
- Team building
- Motivation
- Communication
- Influencing
- Decision making
- Political and cultural awareness
- Negotiation
- Trust building
- Conflict management
- Coaching

While there are additional interpersonal skills that project managers use, the appropriate use of these skills assists the project manager in effectively managing the project.

Project Communications Management
(Chapter 10 of the *PMBOK® Guide*)

161. Answer: A.
PMBOK® Guide, page 287, Introduction; and page 288, Figure 10-1

Project Communications Management
Figure 10-1 provides an overview of the Project Communications Management processes, which are as follows:

10.1 Plan Communications Management—The process of developing an appropriate approach and plan for project communications based on stakeholder's information needs and requirements, and available organizational assets.

10.2 Manage Communications—The process of creating, collecting, distributing, storing, retrieving and the ultimate disposition of project information in accordance with the communications management plan.

10.3 Control Communications—The process of monitoring and controlling communications throughout the entire project life cycle to ensure the information needs of the project stakeholders are met.

162. Answer: A.
PMBOK® Guide, pages 290–291, Section 10.1.1, and page 289, Figure 10-2

Plan Communications Management: Inputs
.1 Project Management Plan
.2 Stakeholder Register
.3 Enterprise Environmental Factors
.4 Organizational Process Assets

163. Answer: D.

PMBOK® Guide, pages 296–297, Section 10.1.3.1

Communications Management Plan

The communications management plan is a component of the project management plan that describes how project communications will be planned, structured, monitored, and controlled. The plan contains the following information:

- Stakeholder communication requirements;
- Information to be communicated, including language, format, content, and level of detail;
- Reason for the distribution of that information;
- Time frame and frequency for the distribution of required information and receipt of acknowledgment or response, if applicable;
- Person responsible for communicating the information;
- Person responsible for authorizing release of confidential information;
- Person or groups who will receive the information;
- Methods or technologies used to convey the information, such as memos, e-mail, and/or press releases;
- Resources allocated for communication activities, including time and budget;
- Escalation process identifying time frames and the management chain (names) for escalation of issues that cannot be resolved at a lower staff level;
- Method for updating and refining the communications management plan as the project progresses and develops;
- Glossary of common terminology;
- Flow charts of the information flow in the project, workflows with possible sequence of authorization, list of reports, and meeting plans, etc.; and
- Communication constraints usually derived from a specific legislation or regulation, technology, and organizational policies, etc.

The communications management plan can also include guidelines and templates for project status meetings, project team meetings, e-meetings, and e-mail messages. The use of a project website and project management software can also be included if these are to be used in the project.

164. Answer: C.
PMBOK® Guide, page 300, Section 10.2.2.4

Information Management Systems
Project information is managed and distributed using a variety of tools, including:
- Hard-copy document management: letters, memos, reports, and press releases;
- Electronic communications management: e-mail, fax, voice mail, telephone, video and web conferencing, websites, and web publishing; and
- Electronic project management tools: web interfaces to scheduling and project management software, meeting and virtual office support software, portals, and collaborative work management tools.

165. Answer: C.
PMBOK® Guide, pages 292–293, Section 10.1.2.2

Communication Technology
The methods used to transfer information among project stakeholders may vary significantly…

Factors that can affect the choice of communication technology include:
- **Urgency of the need for information…**
- **Availability of technology…**
- **Ease of use…**
- **Project environment…**
- **Sensitivity and confidentiality of the information…**

166. Answer: B.

PMBOK® Guide, page 301, Section 10.2.2.5

Performance Reporting

Performance reporting is the act of collecting and distributing performance information, including status reports, progress measurements, and forecasts. Performance reporting involves the periodic collection and analysis of baseline versus actual data to understand and communicate the project progress and performance as well as to forecast the project results.

Performance reporting needs to provide information at an appropriate level for each audience. The format may range from a simple status report to more elaborate reports and may be prepared regularly or on an exception basis. A simple status report might show performance information, such as percent complete or status dashboards for each area (i.e., scope, schedule, cost, and quality). More elaborate reports may include:

- Analysis of past performance,
- Analysis of project forecasts (including time and cost),
- Current status of risks and issues,
- Work completed during the period,
- Work to be completed in the next period,
- Summary of changes approved in the period, and
- Other relevant information, which is reviewed and discussed.

167. Answer: B.

PMBOK® Guide, pages 293–294, Section 10.1.2.3 and Figure 10-4

Communication Models

The communication models used to facilitate communications and the exchange of information may vary from project to project and also within different stages of the same project. A basic communication model, shown in Figure 10-4, consists of two parties, defined as the sender and receiver. Medium is the technology medium and includes the mode of communication, while noise includes any interference or barriers that might compromise the delivery of the message…

The components of the basic communication model need to be considered when project communications are discussed. As part of the communications process, the sender is responsible for the transmission of the message, ensuring the information being communicated is clear and complete, and confirming the communication is correctly understood. The receiver is responsible for ensuring that the information is received in its entirety, understood correctly, and acknowledged or responded to appropriately.

168. Answer: C.

PMBOK® Guide, pages 293–294, Section 10.1.2.3 and
Figure 10-4; and Appendix X3, Section X3.4

Communication Models

...

The components of the basic communication model
need to be considered when project communications
are discussed. As part of the communications process,
the sender is responsible for the transmission
of the message, ensuring the information being
communicated is clear and complete, and confirming
the communication is correctly understood.
The receiver is responsible for ensuring that the
information is received in its entirety, understood
correctly, and acknowledged or responded to
appropriately.

Communication

Listening is an important part of communication.
Listening techniques, both active and passive give the
user insight to problem areas, negotiation and conflict
management strategies, decision making, and problem
resolution.

169. Answer: D.
PMBOK® Guide, pages 292, Section 10.1.2.1

Communication Requirements Analysis

…

Sources of information typically used to identify and define project communication requirements include, but are not limited to:

- Organizational charts;
- Project organization and stakeholder responsibility relationships;
- Disciplines, departments, and specialties involved in the project;
- Logistics of how many persons will be involved with the project and at which locations;
- Internal information needs (e.g., when communicating within organizations);
- External information needs (e.g., when communicating with the media, public, or contractors); and
- Stakeholder information and communication requirements from within the stakeholder register.

170. Answer: A.
PMBOK® Guide, page 301, Section 10.2.2.5

Performance Reporting

Performance reporting is the act of collecting and distributing performance information, including status reports, progress measurements, and forecasts. Performance reporting involves the periodic collection and analysis of baseline versus actual data to understand and communicate the project progress and performance as well as to forecast the project results.

Performance reporting needs to provide information at an appropriate level for each audience. The format may range from a simple status report to more elaborate reports and may be prepared regularly or on an exception basis. A simple status report might show performance information, such as percent complete or status dashboards for each area (i.e., scope, schedule, cost, and quality).

171. Answer: C.
PMBOK® Guide, page 287, Introduction

Project Communications Management
The communication activities involved in these processes may often have many potential dimensions that need to be considered, including, but not limited to:
- Internal (within the project) and external (customer, vendors, other projects, organizations, the public);
- Formal (reports, minutes, briefings) and informal (emails, memos, ad-hoc discussions);
- Vertical (up and down the organization) and horizontal (with peers);
- Official (newsletters, annual report) and unofficial (off the record communications); and
- Written and oral, and verbal (voice inflections) and nonverbal (body language).

172. Answer: C.
PMBOK® Guide, page 300, Section 10.2.2.4

Information Management Systems
Project information is managed and distributed using a variety of tools, including:
- Hard-copy document management: letters, memos, reports, and press releases;
- Electronic communications management: e-mail, fax, voice mail, telephone, video and web conferencing, websites, and web publishing; and
- Electronic project management tools: web interfaces to scheduling and project management software, meeting and virtual office support software, portals, and collaborative work management tools.

173. Answer: A.
PMBOK® Guide, page 292, Section 10.1.2.1

Communication Requirements Analysis
…
The project manager should also consider the number of potential communication channels or paths as an indicator of the complexity of a project's communications. The total number of potential communication channels is n (n − 1)/2, where n represents the number of stakeholders. For example, a project with 10 stakeholders has 10 (10 − 1)/2 = 45 potential communication channels. As a result, a key component of planning the project's actual communications is to determine and limit who will communicate with whom and who will receive what information.

174. Answer: B.
PMBOK® Guide, page 303, Section 10.2.3.4

Lessons learned documentation. Documentation includes the causes of issues, reasoning behind the corrective action chosen, and other types of lessons learned about communications management. Lessons learned need to be documented and distributed so that it becomes part of the historical database for both the project and the performing organization.

175. Answer: D.
PMBOK® Guide, page 298, Section 10.2

Manage Communications
...
Techniques and considerations for effective communications management include, but are not limited to, the following:

- **Sender-receiver models.** Incorporating feedback loops to provide opportunities for interaction/participation and remove barriers to communication.
- **Choice of media.** Situation specifics as to when to communicate in writing versus orally, when to prepare an informal memo versus a formal report, and when to communicate face to face versus by e-mail.
- **Writing style.** Appropriate use of active versus passive voice, sentence structure, and word choice.
- **Meeting management techniques.** Preparing an agenda and dealing with conflicts.
- **Presentation techniques.** Awareness of the impact of body language and design of visual aids.
- **Facilitation techniques.** Building consensus and overcoming obstacles.
- **Listening techniques.** Listening actively (acknowledging, clarifying, and confirming understanding) and removal of barriers that adversely affect comprehension.

176. Answer: B.
PMBOK® Guide, page 303, Section 10.3

Control Communications
Control communications is the process of monitoring and controlling communications throughout the entire project life cycle to ensure the information needs of the project stakeholders are met. The key benefit of this process is that it ensures an optimal information flow among all communication participants, at any moment in time.

Project Risk Management
(Chapter 11 of the *PMBOK® Guide*)

177. Answer: D.
PMBOK® Guide, page 309, Introduction; and page 312, Figure 11-1

Project Risk Management
Project risk management includes the processes of conducting risk management planning, identification, analysis, response planning, and controlling risk on a project. The objectives of project risk management are to increase the likelihood and impact of positive events, and decrease the likelihood and impact of negative events in the project.

Figure 11-1 provides an overview of the Project Risk Management processes, which are as follows:

11.1 Plan Risk Management—The process of defining how to conduct risk management activities for a project.

11.2 Identify Risks—The process of determining which risks may affect the project and documenting their characteristics.

11.3 Perform Qualitative Risk Analysis—The process of prioritizing risks for further analysis or action by assessing and combining their probability of occurrence and impact.

11.4 Perform Quantitative Risk Analysis—The process of numerically analyzing the effect of identified risks on overall project objectives.

11.5 Plan Risk Responses—The process of developing options and actions to enhance opportunities and to reduce threats to project objectives.

11.6 Control Risks—The process of implementing risk response plans, tracking identified risks, monitoring residual risks, identifying new risks, and evaluating risk process effectiveness throughout the project.

178. Answer: B.

PMBOK® Guide, page 311, Introduction

Project Risk Management

...

To be successful, an organization should be committed to address risk management proactively and consistently throughout the project. A conscious choice should be made at all levels of the organization to actively identify and pursue effective risk management during the life of the project. Project risk could exist at the moment a project is initiated. Moving forward on a project without a proactive focus on risk management is likely to lead to more problems arising from unmanaged threats.

179. Answer: A.

PMBOK® Guide, page 344, Section 11.5.2.1

Strategies for Negative Risks or Threats

Three strategies, which typically deal with threats or risks that may have negative impacts on project objectives if they occur, are: *avoid, transfer,* and *mitigate.* The fourth strategy, *accept,* can be used for negative risks or threats as well as positive risks or opportunities. Each of these risk response strategies has varied and unique influence on the risk condition. These strategies should be chosen to match the risk's probability and impact on the project's overall objectives. Avoidance and mitigation strategies are usually good strategies for critical risks with high impact, while transference and acceptance are usually good strategies for threats that are less critical and with low overall impact.

180. **Answer: D.**

PMBOK® Guide, page 344, Section 11.5.2.1

Transfer. Risk transference is a risk response strategy whereby the project team shifts the impact of a threat to a third party, together with ownership of the response. Transferring the risk simply gives another party responsibility for its management—it does not eliminate it. Transferring does not mean disowning the risk by transferring it to a later project or another person without his or her knowledge or agreement. Risk transference nearly always involves payment of a risk premium to the party taking on the risk. Transferring liability for risk is most effective in dealing with financial risk exposure. Transference tools can be quite diverse and include, but are not limited to, the use of insurance, performance bonds, warranties, guarantees, etc. Contracts or agreements may be used to transfer liability for specified risks to another party. For example, when a buyer has capabilities that the seller does not possess, it may be prudent to transfer some work and its concurrent risk contractually back to the buyer. In many cases, use of a cost-plus contract may transfer the cost risk to the buyer, while a fixed-price contract may transfer risk to the seller.

181. Answer: C.

PMBOK® Guide, pages 344–346, Section 11.5.2.1

.1 Strategies for Negative Risks or Threats

...

- **Accept.** Risk acceptance is a risk response strategy whereby the project team decides to acknowledge the risk and not take any action unless the risk occurs. This strategy is adopted where it is not possible or cost-effective to address a specific risk in any other way. This strategy indicates that the project team has decided not to change the project management plan to deal with a risk, or is unable to identify any other suitable response strategy. This strategy can be either passive or active. Passive acceptance requires no action except to document the strategy, leaving the project team to deal with the risks as they occur, and to periodically review the threat to ensure that it does not change significantly. The most common active acceptance strategy is to establish a contingency reserve, including amounts of time, money, or resources to handle the risks.

.2 Strategies for Positive Risks or Opportunities

...

- **Accept.** Accepting an opportunity is being willing to take advantage of the opportunity if it arises, but not actively pursuing it.

182. Answer: A.

PMBOK® Guide, page 327, Section 11.2.3; and page 319, Figure 11-5

Identify Risks: Outputs
.1 Risk Register

The primary output from Identify Risks is the initial entry into the risk register. The risk register is a document in which the results of risk analysis and risk response planning are recorded. It contains the outcomes of the other risk management processes as they are conducted, resulting in an increase in the level and type of information contained in the risk register over time. The preparation of the risk register begins in the Identify Risks process with the following information, and then becomes available to other project management and risk management processes:

- **List of identified risks...**
- **List of potential responses...**

183. Answer: A.

PMBOK® Guide, page 325, Section 11.2.2.3

Checklist Analysis

Risk identification checklists are developed based on historical information and knowledge that has been accumulated from previous similar projects and from other sources of information. The lowest level of the RBS can also be used as a risk checklist. While a checklist may be quick and simple, it is impossible to build an exhaustive one, and care should be taken to ensure the checklist is not used to avoid the effort of proper risk identification. The team should also explore items that do not appear on the checklist. Additionally, the checklist should be pruned from time to time to remove or archive related items. The checklist should be reviewed during project closure to incorporate new lessons learned and improve it for use on future projects.

184. Answer: C.

PMBOK® Guide, pages 321–324, Section 11.2.1; and page 319, Figure 11-5

> **Identify Risks: Inputs**
> .1 Risk Management Plan
> .2 Cost Management Plan
> .3 Schedule Management Plan
> .4 Quality Management Plan
> .5 Human Resource Management Plan
> .6 Scope Baseline
> .7 Activity Cost Estimates
> .8 Activity Duration Estimates
> .9 Stakeholder Register
> .10 Project Documents
> .11 Procurement Documents
> .12 Enterprise Environmental Factors
> .13 Organizational Process Assets

185. Answer: B.

PMBOK® Guide, pages 346–348, Section 11.5.3; and page 342, Figure 11-18

> **Plan Risk Responses: Outputs**
> **.1 Project Management Plan Updates**
> ...
>
> **.2 Project Documents Updates**
> In the Plan Risk Responses process, several project documents are updated as needed. For example, when appropriate risk responses are chosen and agreed upon, they are included in the risk register...

186. Answer: D.

PMBOK® Guide, pages 336–341, Section 11.4.2; and page 334, Figure 11-11

> **Perform Quantitative Risk Analysis: Tools and Techniques**
> **.1 Data Gathering and Representation Techniques**
> **.2 Quantitative Risk Analysis and Modeling Techniques**
> **.3 Expert Judgment**

187. Answer: A.

PMBOK® Guide, page 341, Section 11.4.3; and page 334, Figure 11-11

> **Perform Quantitative Risk Analysis: Outputs**
> **.1 Project Documents Updates**
> Project documents are updated with information resulting from quantitative risk analysis. For example, risk register updates could include:
> - **Probabilistic analysis of the project...**
> - **Probability of achieving cost and time objectives...**
> - **Prioritized list of quantified risks...**
> - **Trends in quantitative risk analysis results...**

188. Answer: D.

PMBOK® Guide, pages 317–318, Section 11.1.3.1 and
Table 11-1; and pages 330–332, Section 11.3.2

Definitions of risk probability and impact. The
quality and credibility of the risk analysis requires
that different levels of risk probability and impact be
defined that are specific to the project context. General
definitions of probability levels and impact levels are
tailored to the individual project during the Plan Risk
Management process for use in subsequent processes.
Table 11-1 is an example of definitions of negative
impacts that could be used in evaluating risk impacts
related to four project objectives. (Similar tables may
be established with a positive impact perspective).
Table 11-1 illustrates both relative and numerical
(in this case, nonlinear) approaches.

Probability and impact matrix. A probability and
impact matrix is a grid for mapping the probability
of each risk occurrence and its impact on project
objectives if that risk occurs. Risks are prioritized
according to their potential implications for having
an effect on the project's objectives. A typical
approach to prioritizing risks is to use a look-up
table or a probability and impact matrix. The specific
combinations of probability and impact that lead to
a risk being rated as "high," "moderate," or "low"
importance are usually set by the organization.

Risk Probability and Impact Assessment
Risk probability assessment investigates the likelihood
that each specific risk will occur. Risk impact
assessment investigates the potential effect on a
project objective such as schedule, cost, quality, or
performance, including both negative effects for
threats and positive effects for opportunities…

Probability and Impact Matrix

Risks can be prioritized for further quantitative analysis and planning risk responses based on their risk rating. Ratings are assigned to risks based on their assessed probability and impact. Evaluation of each risk's importance and priority for attention is typically conducted using a look-up table or a probability and impact matrix. Such a matrix specifies combinations of probability and impact that lead to rating the risks as low, moderate, or high priority. Descriptive terms or numeric values can be used depending on organizational preference.

Each risk is rated on its probability of occurrence and impact on an objective if it does occur. The organization should determine which combinations of probability and impact result in a classification of high risk, moderate risk, and low risk. In a black-and-white matrix, these conditions are denoted using different shades of gray. Specifically in Figure 11-10, the dark gray area (with the largest numbers) represents high risk: the medium gray area (with the smallest numbers) represents low risk, and the light gray area (with in-between numbers) represents moderate risk. Usually, these risk-rating rules are specified by the organization in advance of the project and included in organizational process assets. Risk rating rules can be tailored in the Plan Risk Management process to the specific project.

189. Answer: B.

PMBOK® Guide, pages 353–354, Section 11.6.3; and page 349, Figure 11-20

> **Control Risks: Outputs**
> .1 Work Performance Information
> .2 Change Requests
> .3 Project Management Plan Updates
> .4 Project Document Updates
> .5 Organizational Process Assets Updates

190. Answer: D.

PMBOK® Guide, page 324, Section 11.2.2.2

> **Delphi technique.** The Delphi technique is a way to reach a consensus of experts. Project risk experts participate in this technique anonymously. A facilitator uses a questionnaire to solicit ideas about the important project risks. The responses are summarized and are then recirculated to the experts for further comment. Consensus may be reached in a few rounds of this process. The Delphi technique helps reduce bias in the data and keeps any one person from having undue influence on the outcome.

191. Answer: A.

PMBOK® Guide, pages 331–332, Section 11.3.2.2 and Figure 11-10

Probability and Impact Matrix

Risks can be prioritized for further quantitative analysis and planning risk responses based on their risk rating. Ratings are assigned to risks based on their assessed probability and impact. Evaluation of each risk's importance and priority for attention is typically conducted using a look-up table or a probability and impact matrix. Such a matrix specifies combinations of probability and impact that lead to rating the risks as low, moderate, or high priority. Descriptive terms or numerical values can be used depending on organizational preference.

Each risk is rated on its probability of occurrence and impact on an objective if it does occur. The organization should determine which combinations of probability and impact result in a classification of high risk, moderate risk, and low risk. In a black-and-white matrix, these conditions are denoted using different shades of gray. Specifically in Figure 11-10, the dark gray area (with the largest numbers) represents high risk: the medium gray area (with the smallest numbers) represents low risk, and the light gray area (with in-between numbers) represents moderate risk. Usually, these risk-rating rules are specified by the organization in advance of the project and included in organizational process assets. Risk rating rules can be tailored in the Plan Risk Management process to the specific project.

As illustrated in Figure 11-10, an organization can rate a risk separately for each objective (e.g., cost, time, and scope). In addition, it may develop ways to determine one overall rating for each risk. Finally, opportunities and threats are handled in the same matrix using definitions of the different levels of impact that are appropriate for each.

192. Answer: B.

PMBOK® Guide, page 338, Section 11.4.2.2

Sensitivity analysis. Sensitivity analysis helps to determine which risks have the most potential impact on the project. It helps to understand how the variations in project's objectives correlate with variations in different uncertainties. Conversely, it examines the extent to which the uncertainty of each project element affects the objective being studied when all other uncertain elements are held at their baseline values. One typical display of sensitivity analysis is the tornado diagram (Figure 11-15), which is useful for comparing relative importance and impact of variables that have a high degree of uncertainty to those that are more stable.

193. Answer: C.

PMBOK® Guide, page 337, Section 11.4.2.1; page 339, Section 11.4.2.2 and Figure 11-16; page 343, Section 11.5.2; and Glossary

Probability distributions. Continuous probability distributions, which are used extensively in modeling and simulation, represent the uncertainty in values such as durations of schedule activities and costs of project components. Discrete distributions can be used to represent uncertain events, such as the outcome of a test or a possible scenario in a decision tree.

Expected monetary value analysis. Expected monetary value (EMV) analysis is a statistical concept that calculates the average outcome when the future includes scenarios that may or may not happen (i.e., analysis under uncertainty). The EMV of opportunities are generally expressed as positive values, while those of threats are expressed as negative values. EMV requires a risk-neutral assumption—neither risk averse nor risk seeking. EMV for a project is calculated by multiplying the value of each possible outcome by its probability of occurrence and adding the products together. A common use of this type of analysis is a decision tree analysis (Figure 11-16).

Plan Risk Responses: Tools and Techniques
Several risk response strategies are available. The strategy or mix of strategies most likely to be effective should be selected for each risk. Risk analysis tools, such as decision tree analysis (Section 11.4.2.2), can be used to choose the most appropriate responses.

Decision Tree Analysis. A diagramming and calculation technique for evaluating the implications of a chain of multiple options in the presence of uncertainty.

194. Answer: C.

PMBOK® Guide, pages 316–318, Section 11.1.3.1

Risk Management Plan

The risk management plan is a component of the project management plan and describes how risk management activities will be structured and performed. The risk management plan includes the following:

- **Methodology.**
- **Roles and responsibilities.**
- **Budgeting.**
- **Timing.**
- **Risk categories.**
- **Definitions of risk probability and impact.**
- **Probability and impact matrix.**
- **Revised stakeholders' tolerances.**
- **Reporting formats.**
- **Tracking.**

195. Answer: C.

PMBOK® Guide, pages 328–329, Section 11.3

Perform Qualitative Risk Analysis

Perform Qualitative Risk Analysis is the process of prioritizing risks for further analysis or action by assessing and combining their probability of occurrence and impact. The key benefit of this process is that it enables project managers to reduce the level of uncertainty and to focus on high-priority risks…

Perform Qualitative Risk Analysis assesses the priority of identified risks using their relative probability or likelihood of occurrence, the corresponding impact on project objectives if the risks occur, as well as other factors such as the time frame for response and the organization's risk tolerance associated with the project constraints of cost, schedule, scope, and quality. Such assessments reflect the risk attitude of the project team and other stakeholders…

196. Answer: A.
PMBOK® Guide, page 354, Section 11.6.3.4

Project Documents Updates
Project documents that may be updated as a result of the Control Risk process include, but are not limited to the risk register. Risk register updates may include:

- **Outcomes of risk reassessments, risk audits, and periodic risk reviews.** These outcomes may include identification of new risks, updates to probability, impact, priority, response plans, ownership, and other elements of the risk register. Outcomes can also include closing risks that are no longer applicable and releasing their associated reserves.
- **Actual outcomes of the project's risks and of the risk responses.** This information can help project managers to plan for risk throughout their organizations, as well as on future projects.

197. Answer: C.
PMBOK® Guide, page 339, Section 11.4.2.2

Expected monetary value analysis. Expected monetary value (EMV) analysis is a statistical concept that calculates the average outcome when the future includes scenarios that may or may not happen (i.e., analysis under uncertainty). The EMV of opportunities are generally expressed as positive values, while those of threats are expressed as negative values. EMV requires a risk-neutral assumption—neither risk averse nor risk seeking. EMV for a project is calculated by multiplying the value of each possible outcome by its probability of occurrence and adding the products together. A common use of this type of analysis is a decision tree analysis (Figure 11-16).

198. Answer: B.

PMBOK® Guide, page 326, Section 11.2.2.6

SWOT Analysis

This technique examines the project from each of the strengths, weaknesses, opportunities, and threats (SWOT) perspectives to increase the breadth of identified risks by including internally generated risks. The technique starts with identification of strengths and weaknesses of the organization, focusing on either the project, organization, or the business area in general. SWOT analysis then identifies any opportunities for the project that arise from organizational strengths, and any threats arising from organizational weaknesses. The analysis also examines the degree to which organizational strengths offset threats, as well as identifying opportunities that may serve to overcome weaknesses.

Project Procurement Management

(Chapter 12 of the *PMBOK® Guide*)

199. Answer: C.

PMBOK® Guide, pages 360–364, Section 12.1.1; and page 358, Figure 12-2

Plan Procurement Management: Inputs
.1 Project Management Plan
.2 Requirements Documentation
.3 Risk Register
.4 Activity Resource Requirements
.5 Project Schedule
.6 Activity Cost Estimates
.7 Stakeholder Register
.8 Enterprise Environmental Factors
.9 Organizational Process Assets

200. Answer: A.

PMBOK® Guide, page 368, Section 12.1.3.3

Procurement Documents
Procurement documents are used to solicit proposals from prospective sellers. Terms such as bid, tender, or quotation are generally used when the seller selection decision will be based on price (as when buying commercial or standard items), while a term such as proposal is generally used when other considerations, such as technical capability or technical approach are paramount. Common terms are in use for different types of procurement documents and may include request for information (RFI), invitation for bid (IFB), request for proposal (RFP), request for quotation (RFQ), tender notice, invitation for negotiation, and invitation for seller's initial response. Specific procurement terminology used may vary by industry and location of the procurement.

201. Answer: D.

PMBOK® Guide, page 368, Section 12.1.3.3

Procurement Documents
...
The buyer structures procurement documents to facilitate an accurate and complete response from each prospective seller and to facilitate easy evaluation of the responses. These documents include a description of the desired form of the response, the relevant procurement statement of work (SOW) and any required contractual provisions. With government contracting, some or all of the content and structure of procurement documents may be defined by regulation.

202. Answer: C.

PMBOK® Guide, page 382, Section 12.3.1.4

Approved Change Requests
Approved change requests can include modifications to the terms and conditions of the contract, including the procurement statement of work, pricing, and descriptions of the products, services, or results to be provided. All procurement-related changes are formally documented in writing and approved before being implemented through the Control Procurements process.

203. Answer: B.

PMBOK® Guide, page 376, Section 12.2.2.5

Advertising
Existing lists of potential sellers often can be expanded by placing advertisements in general circulation publications, such as selected newspapers or in specialty trade publications. Some organizations use online resources to communicate solicitations to the vendor community. Some government jurisdictions require public advertising of certain types of procurement items, and most government jurisdictions require public advertising or online posting of pending government contracts.

204. Answer: C.

PMBOK® Guide, page 383, Section 12.3.2.5

Payment Systems

Payments to the seller are typically processed by the accounts payable system of the buyer after certification of satisfactory work by an authorized person on the project team. All payments should be made and documented in strict accordance with the terms of the contract.

205. Answer: A.

PMBOK® Guide, page 389, Section 12.4.3

Closed Procurements

The buyer, usually through its authorized procurement administrator, provides the seller with formal written notice that the contract has been completed. Requirements for formal procurement closure are usually defined in the terms and conditions of the contract and are included in the procurement management plan.

…

Deliverable acceptance. Documentation of formal acceptance of seller-provided deliverables may be required to be retained by the organization. The Close Procurement process ensures this documentation requirement is satisfied. Requirements for formal deliverable acceptance and how to address nonconforming deliverables are usually defined in the agreement.

206. Answer: B.

PMBOK® Guide, page 362, Section 12.1.1.9

> **Fixed-price contracts.** This category of contracts involves setting a fixed total price for a defined product, service, or result to be provided. Fixed-price contracts may also incorporate financial incentives for achieving or exceeding selected project objectives, such as schedule delivery dates, cost and technical performance, or anything that can be quantified and subsequently measured. Sellers under fixed-price contracts are legally obligated to complete such contracts, with possible financial damages if they do not. Under the fixed-price arrangement, buyers need to precisely specify the product or services being procured. Changes in scope may be accommodated, but generally with an increase in contract price.

207. Answer: D.

PMBOK® Guide, page 384, Section 12.3.2.6

> **Claims Administration**
> Contested changes and potential constructive changes are those requested changes where the buyer and seller cannot reach an agreement on compensation for the change or cannot agree that a change has occurred. These contested changes are variously called claims, disputes, or appeals. Claims are documented, processed, monitored, and managed throughout the contract life cycle, usually in accordance with the terms of the contract. If the parties themselves do not resolve a claim, it may have to be handled in accordance with alternative dispute resolution (ADR) typically following procedures established in the contract. Settlement of all claims and disputes through negotiation is the preferred method.

208. Answer: C.
PMBOK® Guide, page 341, Section 12.3.3.2

Change Requests
Change requests to the project management plan, its subsidiary plans, and other components, such as the cost baseline, schedule baseline, and procurement management plan, may result from the Control Procurements process. Change requests are processed for review and approval through the Perform Integrated Change Control process.

Requested but unresolved changes can include direction provided by the buyer or actions taken by the seller, which the other party considers a constructive change to the contract. Since any of these constructive changes may be disputed by one party and can lead to a claim against the other party, such changes are uniquely identified and documented by project correspondence.

209. Answer: A.
PMBOK® Guide, page 388, Section 12.4.2.1

Procurement Audits
A procurement audit is a structured review of the procurement process originating from the Plan Procurement Management process through Control Procurements. The objective of a procurement audit is to identify successes and failures that warrant recognition in the preparation or administration of other procurement contracts on the project, or on other projects within the performing organization.

210. Answer: A.

PMBOK® Guide, pages 362–364, Section 12.1.1.9

All legal contractual relationships generally fall into one of two broad families: either fixed-price or cost reimbursable. Also, there is a third hybrid type commonly in use called the time and materials contract. The more popular contract types in use are discussed below as discrete types, but in practice it is not unusual to combine one or more types into a single procurement.

- **Fixed-price contracts.**
- **Cost-reimbursable contracts.**
- **Time and material contracts (T&M).**

211. Answer: B.

PMBOK® Guide, page 367, Section 12.1.3.2

Procurement Statements of Work

The statement of work (SOW) for each procurement is developed from the project scope baseline and defines only that portion of the project scope that is to be included within the related contract. The procurement SOW describes the procurement item in sufficient detail to allow prospective sellers to determine if they are capable of providing the products, services, or results. Sufficient detail can vary based on the nature of the item, the needs of the buyer, or the expected contract form. Information included in a SOW can include specifications, quantity desired, quality levels, performance data, period of performance, work location, and other requirements.

The procurement SOW is written to be clear, complete, and concise. It includes a description of any collateral services required, such as performance reporting or post-project operational support for the procured item. In some application areas, there are specific content and format requirements for a procurement SOW. Each individual procurement item requires a SOW; however, multiple products or services can be grouped as one procurement item within a single SOW.

The procurement SOW can be revised and refined as required as it moves through the procurement process until incorporated into a signed agreement.

212. Answer: C.

PMBOK® Guide, page 389, Section 12.4.3; and page 386, Figure 12-8

> **Close Procurements: Outputs**
> **.1 Closed Procurements**
> **.2 Organizational Process Assets Updates**
> * **Procurement file.**
> * **Deliverable acceptance.**
> * **Lessons learned documentation.**

213. Answer: D.

PMBOK® Guide, pages 368–369, Section 12.1.3.4

> **Source Selection Criteria**
> Source selection criteria are often included as a part of the procurement documents. Such criteria are developed and used to rate or score seller proposals, and can be objective or subjective.
>
> Selection criteria may be limited to only the purchase price if the procurement item is readily available from a number of acceptable sellers. Purchase price in this context includes both the cost of the item and all ancillary expenses such as delivery.
> …

214. Answer: D.

PMBOK® Guide, pages 375–377, Section 12.2.2; and page 371, Figure 12-4

> **Conduct Procurements: Tools and Techniques**
> **.1 Bidder Conferences**
> **.2 Proposal Evaluation Techniques**
> **.3 Independent Estimates**
> **.4 Expert Judgment**
> **.5 Advertising**
> **.6 Analytical Techniques**
> **.7 Procurement Negotiations**

215. Answer: B.

PMBOK® Guide, page 364, Section 12.1.1.9

Cost Plus Fixed Fee Contracts (CPFF). The seller is reimbursed for all allowable costs for performing the contract work, and receives a fixed-fee payment calculated as a percentage of the initial estimated project costs. A fee is paid only for completed work and does not change due to seller performance. Fee amounts do not change unless the project scope changes.

216. Answer: A.

PMBOK® Guide, page 365, Section 12.1.2.1

Make-or-Buy Analysis

A make-or-buy analysis is a general management technique used to determine whether particular work can best be accomplished by the project team or should be purchased from outside sources. Sometimes a capability may exist within the project organization, but may be committed to working on other projects, in which case, the project may need to source such effort from outside the organization in order to meet its schedule commitments.

Budget constraints may influence make-or-buy decisions. If a buy decision is to be made, then a further decision of whether to purchase or lease is also made. A make-or-buy analysis should consider all related costs—both direct costs as well as indirect support costs. For example, the buy-side of the analysis includes both the actual out-of-pocket costs to purchase the product, as well as the indirect costs of supporting the purchasing process and purchased item.

Available contract types are also considered during the buy analysis. The risk sharing between the buyer and seller determines the suitable contract types, while the specific contract terms and conditions formalize the degree of risk being assumed by the buyer and seller. Some jurisdictions have other types of contracts defined, for example, contract types based on the obligations of the seller—not the customer—and the contract parties have the obligation to identify the appropriate type of contract as soon as the applicable law has been agreed upon.

Stakeholder Management
(Chapter 13 of the *PMBOK® Guide*)

217. Answer: B.
PMBOK® Guide, page 393, Section 13.1

Identify Stakeholders
Identify stakeholders is the process of identifying the people, groups, or organizations that could impact or be impacted by a decision, activity, or outcome of the project, analyzing and documenting relevant information regarding their interests, involvement, interdependencies, influence, and potential impact on project success. The key benefit of this process is that it allows the project manager to identify the appropriate focus for each stakeholder or group of stakeholders.

218. Answer: A.
PMBOK® Guide, page 391, Section 13.1 and last paragraph

Identify Stakeholders
The process of identifying the people, groups, or organizations that could impact or be impacted by a decision, activity, or outcome of the project; and analyzing and documenting relevant information regarding their interests, involvement, interdependencies, influence, and potential impact on project success.

...

Every project will have stakeholders who are impacted by or can impact the project in a positive or negative way. While some stakeholders may have a limited ability to influence the project, others may have significant influence on the project and its expected outcomes. The ability of the project manager to correctly identify and manage these stakeholders in an appropriate manner can mean the difference between success and failure.

219. Answer: C.
PMBOK® Guide, page 394, Section 13.1 and page 404, Section 13.3

Identify Stakeholders
It is critical for project success to identify the stakeholders early in the project or phase and to analyze their levels of interest, their individual expectations, as well as their importance and influence. This initial assessment should be reviewed and updated regularly.

Manage Stakeholder Engagement
Manage Stakeholder Engagement is the process of communicating and working with stakeholders to meet their needs/expectations, address issues as they occur, and foster appropriate stakeholder engagement in project activities throughout the project life cycle. The key benefit of this process is that it allows the project manager to increase support and minimize resistance from stakeholders, significantly increasing the chances to achieve project success.

220. Answer: C.
PMBOK® Guide, page 391, Section 13.2

Plan Stakeholder Management
The process of developing appropriate management strategies to effectively engage stakeholders throughout the project life cycle, based on the analysis of their needs, interests, and potential impact on project success.

221. Answer: A.
PMBOK® Guide, page 391, Section 13.3

Manage Stakeholder Engagement
The process of communicating and working with stakeholders to meet their needs/expectations, address issues as they occur, and foster appropriate stakeholder engagement in project activities throughout the project life cycle.

222. Answer: D.
PMBOK® Guide, page 391, Section 13.4

Control Stakeholder Engagement
The process of monitoring overall project stakeholder relationships and adjusting strategies and plans for engaging stakeholders.

223. Answer: C.
PMBOK® Guide, page 396, Section 13.1.2.1

Stakeholder Analysis
...
There are multiple classification models used for stakeholders analysis, such as:
- *Power/interest grid*, grouping the stakeholders based on their level of authority ("power") and their level or concern ("interest") regarding the project outcomes;

224. Answer: D.
PMBOK® Guide, page 398, Section 13.1.3.1

Stakeholder Register
The main output of the Identify Stakeholders process is the stakeholder register. This contains all details related to the identified stakeholders including, but not limited to:
- **Identification information.** Name, organizational position, location, role in the project, contact information;
- **Assessment information.** Major requirements, main expectations, potential influence in the project, phase in the life cycle with the most interest; and
- **Stakeholder classification.** Internal/external, supporter/neutral/resistor, etc.

The stakeholder register should be consulted and updated on a regular basis, as stakeholders may change—or new ones identified—throughout the life cycle of the project.

225. Answer: D.
PMBOK® Guide, page 402, Section 13.2.2.3

Analytical Techniques
The current engagement level of all stakeholders needs to be compared to the planned engagement levels required for successful project completion. Stakeholder engagement throughout the life cycle of the project is critical to project success.

The engagement level of the stakeholders can be classified as follows:
- **Unaware.** Unaware of project and potential impacts.
- **Resistant.** Aware of project and potential impacts and resistant to change.
- **Neutral.** Aware of project yet neither supportive nor resistant.
- **Supportive.** Aware of project and potential impacts and supportive to change.
- **Leading.** Aware of project and potential impacts and actively engaged in ensuring the project is a success.

226. Answer: B.
PMBOK® Guide, page 405, Section 13.3

Manage Stakeholder Engagement
Manage stakeholder engagement involves activities such as:
- Engaging stakeholders at appropriate project stages to obtain or confirm their continued commitment to the success of the project;
- Managing stakeholder expectations through negotiation and communication, ensuring project goals are achieved;
- Addressing potential concerns that have not yet become issues and anticipating future problems that may be raised by stakeholders. Such concerns need to be identified and discussed as soon as possible to assess associated project risks; and
- Clarifying and resolving issues that have been identified.

227. Answer: C.
PMBOK® Guide, page 406, Section 13.3

Manage Stakeholder Engagement
Managing stakeholder engagement helps to increase the probability of project success by ensuring that stakeholders clearly understand the project goals, objectives, benefits, and risks. This enables them to be active supporters of the project and to help guide activities and project decisions. By anticipating people's reactions to the project, proactive actions can be taken to win support or minimize negative impacts.

The ability of stakeholders to influence the project is typically highest during the initial stages and gets progressively lower as the project progresses. The project manager is responsible for engaging and managing the various stakeholders in a project and may call upon the project sponsor to assist as needed. Active management of stakeholder involvement decreases the risk of the project failing to meet its goals and objectives.

228. Answer: D.
PMBOK® Guide, pages 412–413, Section 13.4.2

Control Stakeholder Engagement: Tools and Techniques
13.4.2.1 Information Management Systems
...
13.4.2.2 Expert Judgment
...
13.4.2.3 Meetings
...

229. Answer: A.

PMBOK® Guide, page 413, Section 13.4.2.3

Meetings
Status review meetings are used to exchange and
analyze information about stakeholder engagement.

230. Answer: B.

PMBOK® Guide, page 396, Section 13.1.2.1 and page 397,
Figure 13-4

Stakeholder Analysis
…
There are multiple classification models used for
stakeholders analysis, such as:
- *Power/interest grid*, grouping the stakeholders
  based on their level of authority ("power") and their
  level or concern ("interest") regarding the project
  outcomes;

231. Answer: C.

PMBOK® Guide, page 396, Section 13.1.2.1 and page 397, Figure 13-4

Stakeholder Analysis

...

There are multiple classification models used for stakeholders analysis, such as:

- *Power/interest grid*, grouping the stakeholders based on their level of authority ("power") and their level or concern ("interest") regarding the project outcomes;
- *Power/influence grid*, grouping the stakeholders based on their level of authority ("power") and their active involvement ("influence") in the project;
- *Influence/impact grid*, grouping the stakeholders based on their active involvement ("influence") in the project and their ability to effect changes to the project's planning or execution ("impact"); and
- *Salience model*, describing classes of stakeholders based on their power (ability to impose their will), urgency (need for immediate attention), and legitimacy (their involvement is appropriate).

Appendix X3
(Interpersonal Skills)

232. Answer: D.
PMBOK® Guide, Appendix X3, Section X3.1; and page 284, Section 9.4.2.4

Leadership
Leadership involves focusing the efforts of a group of people toward a common goal and enabling them to work as a team. In general terms, leadership is the ability to get things done through others. Respect and trust, rather than fear and submission, are the key elements of effective leadership. Although important throughout all project phases, effective leadership is critical during the beginning phases of a project when the emphasis is on communicating the vision and motivating and inspiring project participants to achieve high performance.

Leadership. Successful projects require strong leadership skills. Leadership is important through all phases of the project life cycle. There are multiple leadership theories defining leadership styles that should be used as needed for each situation or team. It is especially important to communicate the vision and inspire the project team to achieve high performance.

233. Answer: B.
PMBOK® Guide, Appendix X3, Section X3.2; and page 276, Section 9.3.2.3

Team Building
Team building is the process of helping a group of individuals, bound by a common purpose, to work with each other, the leader, external stakeholders, and the organization. The result of good leadership and good team building is teamwork.

Team-building activities consist of tasks (establish goals, define, and negotiate roles, responsibilities, and procedures) and processes (interpersonal behavior with emphasis on communication, conflict management, motivation, and leadership). Developing a team environment involves handling project team problems and discussing these as team issues without placing blame on individuals. Team building can be further enhanced by obtaining top management support; encouraging team member commitment; introducing appropriate rewards, recognition, and ethics; creating a team identity; managing conflicts effectively; promoting trust and open communication among team members; and providing leadership.

Team-Building Activities
As an ongoing process, team building is crucial to project success. While team building is essential during the initial stages of a project, it is a never-ending process. Changes in a project environment are inevitable, and to manage them effectively, a continued or a renewed team-building effort should be applied. The project manager should continually monitor team functionality and performance to determine if any actions are needed to prevent or correct various team problems.

234. Answer: C.

PMBOK® Guide, Appendix X3, Section X3.3; and page 277, Section 9.3.2.6

Motivation

...

Motivating in a project environment involves creating an environment to meet project objectives while providing maximum satisfaction related to what people value most. These values may include job satisfaction, challenging work, a sense of accomplishment, achievement and growth, sufficient financial compensation, and other rewards and recognition the individual considers necessary and important.

Recognition and Rewards

. . .

People are motivated if they feel they are valued in the organization and this value is demonstrated by the rewards given to them. Generally, money is viewed as a tangible aspect of any reward system, but intangible rewards could be equally or even more effective. Most project team members are motivated by an opportunity to grow, accomplish, and apply their professional skills to meet new challenges. A good strategy for project managers is to give the team recognition throughout the life cycle of the project rather than waiting until the project is completed.

235. Answer: A.
PMBOK® Guide, Appendix X3, Section X3.4; and page 287, Introduction

Communication

...

To communicate effectively, the project manager should be aware of the communication styles of other parties, cultural nuances/norms, relationships, personalities, and the overall context of the situation. Awareness of these factors leads to mutual understanding and thus to effective communication. Project managers should identify various communication channels, understand what information they need to provide, what information they need to receive, and which interpersonal skills will help them communicate effectively with various project stakeholders. Carrying out team-building activities to determine team member communications styles (e.g., directive, collaborative, logical, explorer, etc.), allows managers to plan their communications with appropriate sensitivity to relationships and cultural differences.

Listening is an important part of communication. Listening techniques, both active and passive give the user insight to problem areas, negotiation and conflict management strategies, decision making, and problem resolution.

Project Communications Management

Project communications management includes the processes that are required to ensure timely and appropriate planning, collection, creation, distribution, storage, retrieval, management, control, monitoring, and the ultimate disposition of project information. Project managers spend most of their time communicating with team members and other project stakeholders, whether they are internal (at all organizational levels) or external to the organization. Effective communication creates a bridge between diverse stakeholders who may have different cultural and organizational backgrounds, different levels of expertise, and different perspectives and interests, which impact or have an influence upon the project execution or outcome.

236. Answer: C.

PMBOK® Guide, Appendix X3, Section X3.7; and pages 20–21, Section 2.1.1

Political and Cultural Awareness

… Cultural differences can be both individual and corporate in nature and may involve both internal and external stakeholders. An effective way to manage this cultural diversity is through getting to know the various team members and the use of good communication planning as part of the overall project plan.

Culture at a behavioral level includes those behaviors and expectations that occur independently of geography, ethnic heritage, or common and disparate languages. Culture can impact the speed of working, the decision-making process, and the impulse to act without appropriate planning. This may lead to conflict and stress in some organizations, thereby affecting the performance of project managers and project teams.

Organizational Cultures and Styles

Organizations are systematic arrangements of entities (persons and/or departments) aimed at accomplishing a purpose, which may involve undertaking projects. An organization's culture and style affect how it conducts projects. Cultures and styles are group phenomena known as cultural norms, which develop over time. The norms include established approaches to initiating and planning projects, the means considered acceptable for getting the work done, and recognized authorities who make or influence decisions.

Organizational culture is shaped by the common experiences of members of the organization and most organizations have developed unique cultures over time by practice and common usage …

In light of globalization, understanding the impact of cultural influences is critical in projects involving diverse organizations and locations around the world. Culture becomes a critical factor in defining project success, and multi-cultural competence becomes critical for the project manager.

Glossary

237. Answer: B.
PMBOK® Guide, Glossary; and page 345, Section 11.5.2.1

> **Acceptance Criteria.** A set of conditions that is required to be met before deliverables are accepted.

> **Performance Measurement Baseline.** An approved, integrated scope-schedule-cost plan for the project work against which project execution is compared to measure and manage performance. The PMB includes contingency reserve, but excludes management reserve.

> **Accept.** ... This strategy can be either passive or active. Passive acceptance requires no action except to document the strategy, leaving the project team to deal with the risks as they occur, and to periodically review the threat to ensure that it does not change significantly. The most common active acceptance strategy is to establish a contingency reserve, including amounts of time, money, or resources to handle the risks.

238. Answer: A.
PMBOK® Guide, Glossary

> **Code of Accounts.** A numbering system used to uniquely identify each component of the work breakdown structure (WBS).

239. Answer: C.
PMBOK® Guide, Glossary

> **Baseline.** The approved version of a work product that can be changed only through formal change control procedures and is used as a basis for comparison.

> **Cost Baseline.** The approved version of the time-phased project budget, excluding any management reserves, which can be changed only through formal change control procedures and is used as a basis for comparison to actual results.

240. Answer: D.
PMBOK® Guide, Glossary

> **Scope Management Plan.** A component of the project or program management plan that describes how the scope will be defined, developed, monitored, controlled, and verified.

241. Answer: A.
PMBOK® Guide, Glossary

> **Project Scope Statement.** The description of the project scope, major deliverables, assumptions, and constraints.

242. Answer: B.

PMBOK® Guide, Glossary; and page 132, Section 5.4.3.1

> **Work Package.** The work defined at the lowest level of the work breakdown structure for which cost and duration can be estimated and managed.

> **Control Account.** A management control point where scope, budget, actual cost, and schedule are integrated and compared to earned value for performance measurement.

> **WBS.** … A control account is a management control point where scope, budget, actual cost, and schedule are integrated and compared to the earned value for performance measurement. Control accounts are placed at selected management points in the WBS. Each control account may include one or more work packages, but each of the work packages should be associated with only one control account.

243. Answer: C.

PMBOK® Guide, Glossary

> **Float.** Also called slack. See *total float* and *free float*.

> **Free Float.** The amount of time that a schedule activity can be delayed without delaying the early start date of any successor or violating a schedule constraint.

> **Total Float.** The amount of time that a schedule activity can be delayed or extended from its early start date without delaying the project finish date or violating a schedule constraint.

244. Answer: A.

PMBOK® Guide, Glossary

Performance Measurement Baseline. An approved, integrated scope-schedule-cost plan for the project work against which project execution is compared to measure and manage performance. The PMB includes contingency reserve, but excludes management reserve.

245. Answer: D.

PMBOK® Guide, Glossary

Cost of Quality. A method of determining the costs incurred to ensure quality. Prevention and appraisal costs (cost of conformance) include costs for quality planning, quality control (QC), and quality assurance to ensure compliance to requirements (i.e., training, QC systems, etc.). Failure costs (cost of nonconformance) include costs to rework products, components, or processes that are non-compliant, costs of warranty work and waste, and loss of reputation.

246. Answer: B.

PMBOK® Guide, Glossary

Common Acronyms
FFP   firm fixed price contract

Firm-Fixed-Price Contract (FFP). A type of fixed price contract where the buyer pays the seller a set amount (as defined by the contract), regardless of the seller's costs.

247. Answer: B.
PMBOK® Guide, Glossary; page 78, Section 4.2.3.1; and page 96, Section 4.5

> **Baseline.** The approved version of a work product that can be changed only through formal change control procedures and is used as a basis for comparison.

> … Once the project management plan is baselined, it may only be changed when a change request is generated and approved through the Perform Integrated Change Control process.

> … The project management plan, the project scope statement, and other deliverables are maintained by carefully and continuously managing changes, either by rejecting changes or by approving changes, thereby assuring that only approved changes are incorporated into a revised baseline.

248. Answer: D.
PMBOK® Guide, Glossary; and page 13, Section 1.5.1

> **Product Life Cycle.** The series of phases that represent the evolution of a product, from concept through delivery, growth, maturity, and to retirement.

> **Project Life Cycle.** The series of phases that a project passes through from its initiation to its closure.

> Operations are ongoing endeavors that produce repetitive outputs, with resources assigned to do basically the same set of tasks according to the standards institutionalized in a product life cycle. Unlike the ongoing nature of operations, projects are temporary endeavors.

249. Answer: C.
PMBOK® Guide, Glossary; and page 55, Section 3.4

Progressive Elaboration. The iterative process of increasing the level of detail in a project management plan as greater amounts of information and more accurate estimates become available.

… The complex nature of project management may require the use of repeated feedback loops for additional analysis. As more project information or characteristics are gathered and understood, additional planning will likely be required. Significant changes occurring throughout the project life cycle trigger a need to revisit one or more of the planning processes and possibly some of the initiating processes. This progressive detailing of the project management plan is called progressive elaboration, indicating that planning and documentation are iterative and ongoing activities.

250. Answer: A.
PMBOK® Guide, Glossary; and page 353, Section 11.6.3.2

Workaround. A response to a threat that has occurred, for which a prior response had not been planned or was not effective.

Recommended corrective actions. These are activities that realign the performance of the project work with the project management plan. They include contingency plans and workarounds. The latter are responses that were not initially planned, but are required to deal with emerging risks that were previously unidentified or accepted passively.